How to Use This Book

Look for these special features in this book:

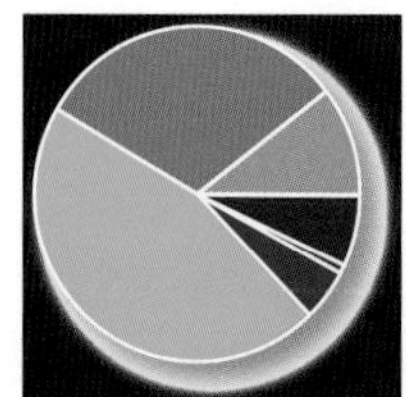

SIDEBARS, **CHARTS**, **GRAPHS**, and original **MAPS** expand your understanding of what's being discussed—and also make useful sources for classroom reports.

FAQs answer common **F**requently **A**sked **Q**uestions about people, places, and things.

WOW FACTORS offer "Who knew?" facts to keep you thinking.

TRAVEL GUIDE gives you tips on exploring the state—either in person or right from your chair!

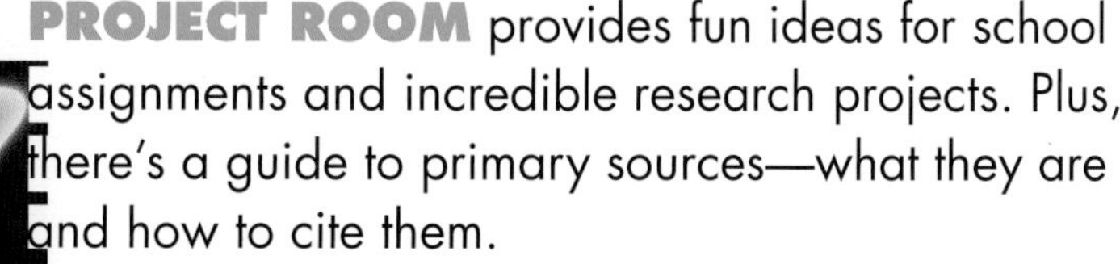

PROJECT ROOM provides fun ideas for school assignments and incredible research projects. Plus, there's a guide to primary sources—what they are and how to cite them.

Please note: All statistics are as up-to-date as possible at the time of publication.

Consultants: Joel D. Blum, Professor of Geological Sciences, University of Michigan; Leonard A. Coombs, Acquisitions Archivist, Bentley Historical Library, University of Michigan; William Loren Katz

Book production by The Design Lab

Library of Congress Cataloging-in-Publication Data
Raatma, Lucia.
Michigan / by Lucia Raatma.
p. cm.—(America the beautiful. Third series)
Includes bibliographical references and index.
ISBN-13: 978-0-531-18562-9
ISBN-10: 0-531-18562-1
1. Michigan—Juvenile literature. I. Title. II. Series.
F566.3.R33 2008
977.4—dc22 2006100708

1 2 3 4 5 6 7 8 9 10 R 17 16 15 14 13 12 11 10 09 08

Michigan

BY LUCIA RAATMA

Third Series

Children's Press®
An Imprint of Scholastic Inc.
New York ★ Toronto ★ London ★ Auckland ★ Sydney
Mexico City ★ New Delhi ★ Hong Kong
Danbury, Connecticut

CONTENTS

1 LAND

Learn about Great Lakes and wild weather, trumpeter swans and wildlife conservation. . . **8**

2 FIRST PEOPLE

Read all about the early people who hunted, fished, farmed, made canoes, and settled in villages. **20**

3 EXPLORATION AND SETTLEMENT

Explore missions at Sault Sainte Marie and the Straits of Mackinac, the fur trade, and how the territory gained freedom from Great Britain. . . . **26**

6 PEOPLE

Find out how Michiganians talk and eat, and meet singers and writers, artists and athletes. **62**

7 GOVERNMENT

Learn about the legislature in Lansing, the Youth in Government program, and the state flag and seal. **76**

8 ECONOMY

Find out about running farms and making breakfast cereal, building cars and booming businesses. **90**

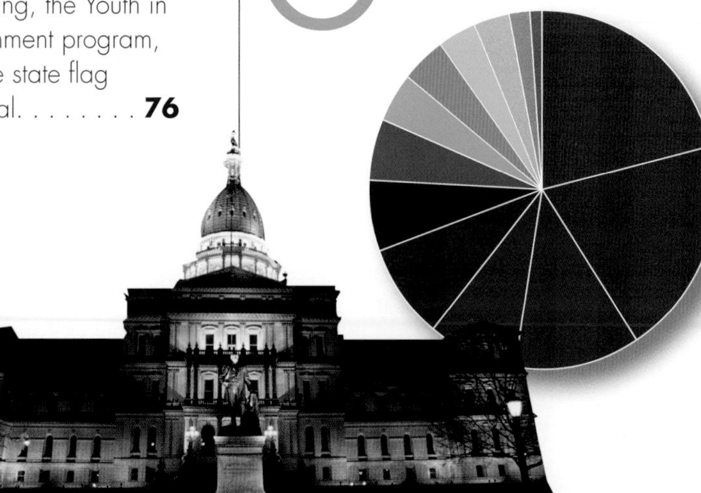

4 GROWTH AND CHANGE

Michigan fights the War of 1812, becomes a state, and plays a role in the Civil War. . . **34**

MORE MODERN TIMES

5 See how the state reacted to the Great Depression and World War II, labor unions, and the Great Migration. **50**

9 TRAVEL GUIDE

Visit the Upper and Lower Peninsulas, and tour museums, historic towns, and picturesque islands. **104**

PROJECT ROOM

★

PROJECTS 116

TIMELINE 122

GLOSSARY 125

FAST FACTS 126

BIOGRAPHICAL DICTIONARY. . .133

RESOURCES 137

★

INDEX 139

AUTHOR'S TIPS AND SOURCE NOTES. 143

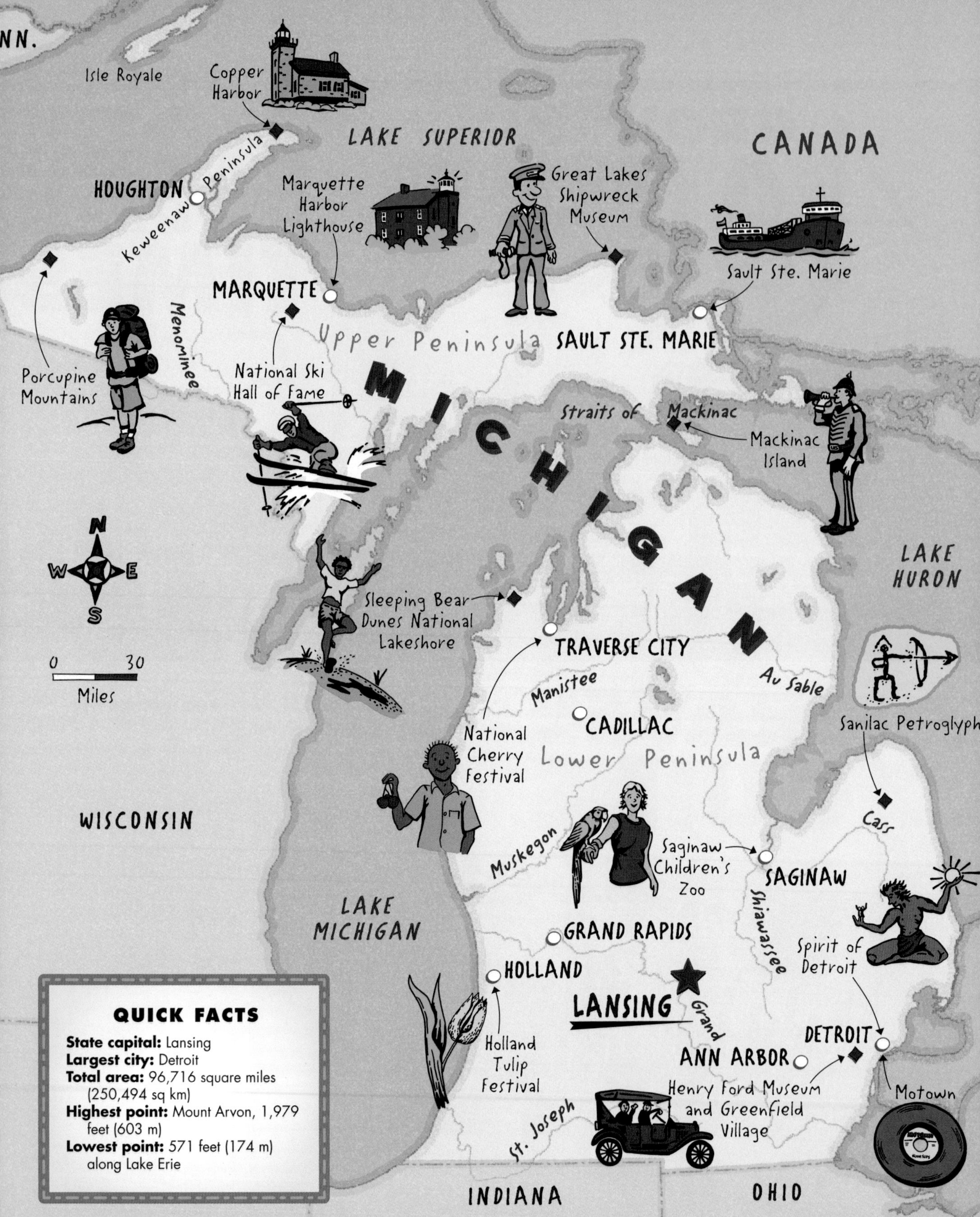

MINN.
Isle Royale
Copper Harbor
LAKE SUPERIOR
CANADA
HOUGHTON
Keweenaw Peninsula
Marquette Harbor Lighthouse
Great Lakes Shipwreck Museum
Sault Ste. Marie
MARQUETTE
SAULT STE. MARIE
Upper Peninsula
Menominee
Porcupine Mountains
National Ski Hall of Fame
MICHIGAN
Straits of Mackinac
Mackinac Island
LAKE HURON
Sleeping Bear Dunes National Lakeshore
TRAVERSE CITY
Au Sable
Manistee
CADILLAC
Sanilac Petroglyph
National Cherry Festival
Lower Peninsula
0 30
Miles
WISCONSIN
Cass
Muskegon
Saginaw Children's Zoo
SAGINAW
Shiawassee
LAKE MICHIGAN
GRAND RAPIDS
Spirit of Detroit
HOLLAND
LANSING
Grand
DETROIT
ANN ARBOR
Holland Tulip Festival
Henry Ford Museum and Greenfield Village
Motown
St. Joseph
INDIANA
OHIO
N
W
E
S
QUICK FACTS
State capital: Lansing
Largest city: Detroit
Total area: 96,716 square miles (250,494 sq km)
Highest point: Mount Arvon, 1,979 feet (603 m)
Lowest point: 571 feet (174 m) along Lake Erie

Welcome to Michigan!

HOW DID MICHIGAN GET ITS NAME?

Michigan comes from the Ojibwa word *michigama*, sometimes spelled *meicigama*, which means "great lake." French explorers heard this term when they came to the area and began using it to refer to what is now Lake Michigan, one of the four Great Lakes that border the state. When the U.S. Congress created the Territory of Michigan in 1805, it also became the official name of the land.

READ ABOUT

A State in Two Parts 10

Land Regions 12

Climate 14

Plant Life 15

Animal Life 16

Saving Resources 17

Michigan's Tahquamenon Falls in autumn

LAND

★

POUNDING WATERFALLS, RUSHING STREAMS, LAZY RIVERS, STUNNING LAKES—ALL THIS WATER MAKES MICHIGAN A "WATER WONDERLAND," WHICH IS ONE OF ITS NICKNAMES. Within the state's 96,716 square miles (250,494 square kilometers), there are 199 waterfalls and more than 11,000 inland lakes. From its highest point at Mount Arvon, which is 1,979 feet (603 meters), to its lowest point of 571 feet (174 m) along Lake Erie, Michigan is home to stunning land features and a variety of plants and animals.

A STATE IN TWO PARTS

WORD TO KNOW

peninsula *a body of land surrounded by water on three sides but connected to a larger piece of land*

Michigan is located in the north-central part of the United States, just south of Canada. The state is split into two parts: the Upper **Peninsula** (the northern part) and the Lower Peninsula (the southern part). Because of its shape, the Lower Peninsula is sometimes called the mitten. The little peninsula north of Detroit is known as the mitten's thumb.

What caused these two sections of land and neighboring islands to form as they did? What is now Michigan has two different kinds of rock beneath it. Under the Upper Peninsula is an ancient and very hard rock formation called the Canadian Shield. This rock formation covers most of eastern and central Canada, and it extends southward into the Upper Peninsula. Under the Lower Peninsula are softer sedimentary rocks that

Michigan Geo-Facts

Along with the state's geographical highlights, this chart ranks Michigan's land, water, and total area compared to all other states.

Total area; rank	96,716 square miles (250,494 sq km); 11th
Land; rank	56,804 square miles (147,122 sq km); 22nd
Water; rank	39,912 square miles (103,372 sq km); 2nd
Inland water	1,611 square miles (4,172 sq km); 13th
Great Lakes	38,301 square miles (99,200 sq km); 1st
Geographic center	In Wexford County, 5 miles (8 km) northwest of Cadillac
Latitude	41° 41′ N to 48° 15′ N
Longitude	82° 26′ W to 90° 31′ W
Highest point	Mount Arvon, 1,979 feet (603 m)
Lowest point	571 feet (174 m) along Lake Erie
Largest city	Detroit
Longest river	Grand River, 260 miles (418 km)

Source: U.S. Census Bureau

Michigan isn't very big or very small. Its land area ranks 22nd in the list of U.S. states. The state of Delaware could fit inside it more than 38 times.

The Mackinac Bridge (top left) rises high over the icy Straits of Mackinac to connects the Upper and Lower Peninsulas.

were deposited into an ancient sea that existed in the area of Michigan hundreds of millions of years ago. Ice sheets swept down from what is now northern Canada, and tongues of ice eroded large troughs in the softer rocks on either side of the Lower Peninsula, which later became Lakes Michigan, Huron, and Erie. When the ice sheets began to melt, sediment that had been carried by the glaciers from lands far to the north was deposited across Michigan. When the last of the ice retreated from the area about 4,000 years ago, the troughs that had been eroded by tongues of ice flooded with water. This formed the two peninsulas, the Great Lakes, and the islands in these lakes.

The **Straits** of Mackinac (pronounced MACK-in-aw), which link Lake Huron and Lake Michigan, divide the two peninsulas. The Mackinac Bridge connects the peninsulas, soaring above the straits.

WORD TO KNOW

straits *narrow passageways of water that connect larger bodies of water*

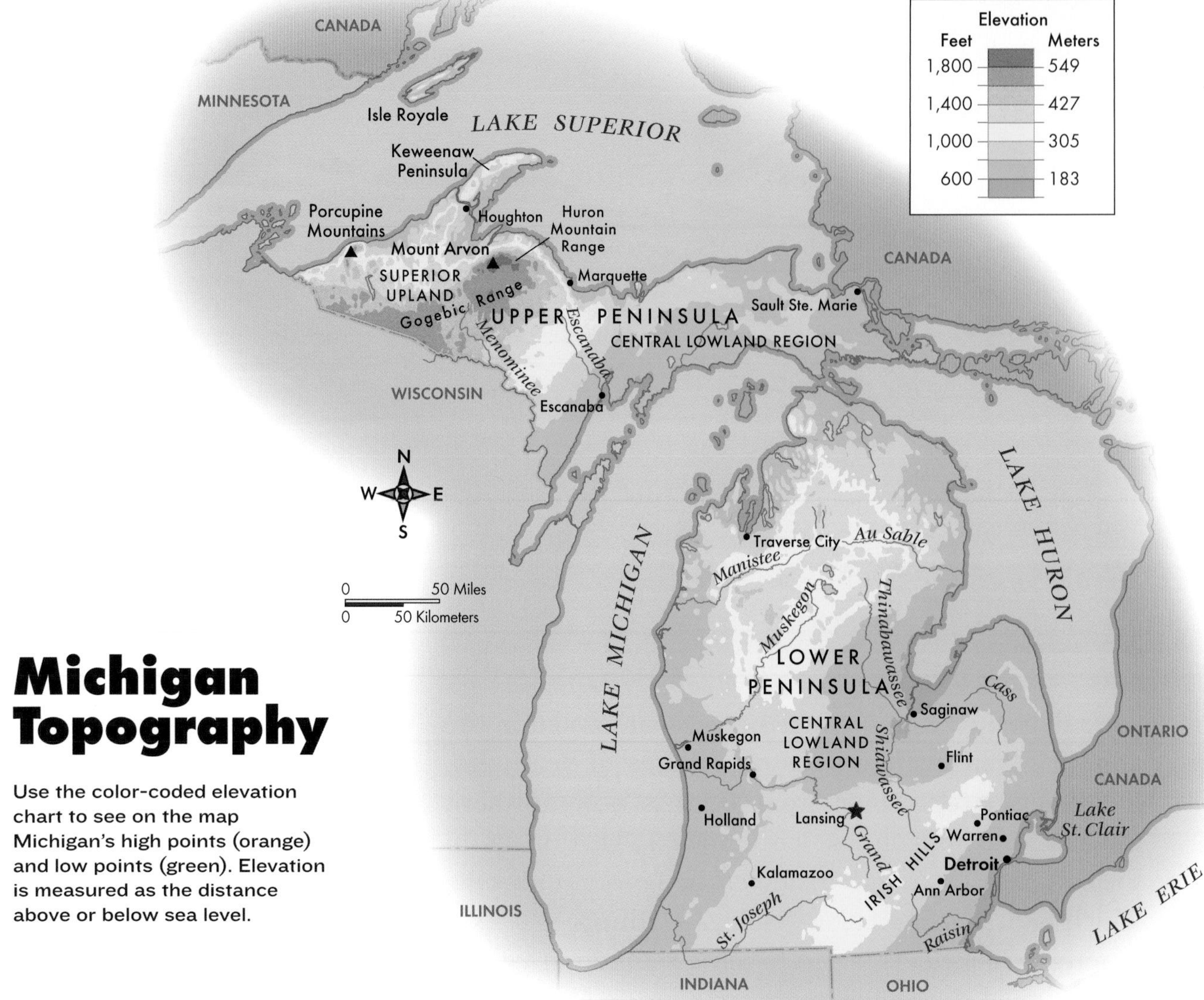

Michigan Topography

Use the color-coded elevation chart to see on the map Michigan's high points (orange) and low points (green). Elevation is measured as the distance above or below sea level.

LAND REGIONS

A section of the northern part of the Upper Peninsula touches Canada's Ontario Province, and Wisconsin borders to the south. To the south of the Lower Peninsula, you'll find Indiana and Ohio. The Lower Peninsula is bordered on the east by Ontario. Two geographic regions make up the two peninsulas: the Superior Upland and the Central Lowland.

The Superior Upland

Rugged hills and forests make up the Superior Upland. This area lies in the western part of the Upper Peninsula. It is home to some of the nation's biggest deposits of iron and copper. Here you'll find the Porcupine and the Huron mountain ranges. The Huron Range includes Mount Arvon, which is the highest point in the state at 1,979 feet (603 m). But get this: Mount Curwood, only 5 miles (8 km) away, was considered the highest point in the state until 1982, when a new survey confirmed that Mount Arvon is 1 foot (0.3 m) taller!

Michigan's shoreline totals 3,288 miles (5,292 km)—more than any other state except Alaska.

The Central Lowland

Thousands of years ago, ice covered what is now the Central Lowland. When it melted, the soil that was left behind was very fertile—perfect for growing crops. This region covers all of the Lower Peninsula and the eastern part of the Upper Peninsula. It is made up of farmland, rolling hills, and sand dunes, including 35 miles (56 km) along the shores of Lake Michigan called the Sleeping Bear Dunes National Lakeshore.

Sleeping Bear Dunes National Lakeshore includes 35 miles (56 km) of Lake Michigan shoreline.

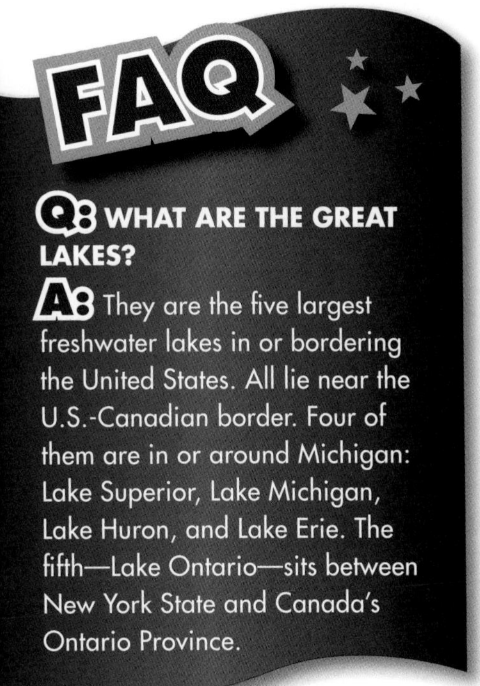

Q: WHAT ARE THE GREAT LAKES?

A: They are the five largest freshwater lakes in or bordering the United States. All lie near the U.S.-Canadian border. Four of them are in or around Michigan: Lake Superior, Lake Michigan, Lake Huron, and Lake Erie. The fifth—Lake Ontario—sits between New York State and Canada's Ontario Province.

ALL THAT WATER

Four of the five Great Lakes—Michigan, Huron, Erie, and Superior—are part of Michigan. Lake Superior covers about 31,700 square miles (82,100 sq km), making it the largest freshwater lake in the world. One of Michigan's several nicknames is The Great Lakes State.

Michigan has lots of water, but it isn't just in the four Great Lakes. Some of its other big lakes are Lake Gogebic in the Upper Peninsula and Houghton, Crystal, and Torch lakes in the Lower Peninsula. The longest river is the Grand River at 260 miles (418 km). It snakes through the central part of the state and empties into Lake Michigan at Grand Haven.

CLIMATE

Michigan's summers are warm and sunny. Its springs are mild, and its autumns are crisp and cool. But its winters? Well, those are a different story. Expect rain, sleet, hail, snow, and even blizzards.

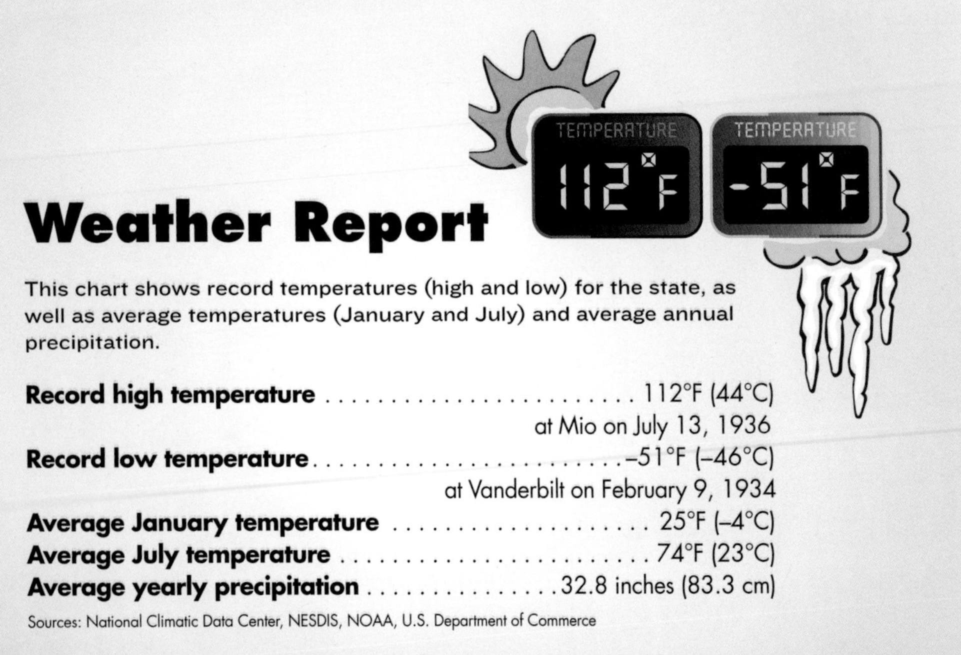

Weather Report

This chart shows record temperatures (high and low) for the state, as well as average temperatures (January and July) and average annual precipitation.

Record high temperature . . . . 112°F (44°C) at Mio on July 13, 1936

Record low temperature . . . . –51°F (–46°C) at Vanderbilt on February 9, 1934

Average January temperature . . . . 25°F (–4°C)

Average July temperature . . . . 74°F (23°C)

Average yearly precipitation . . . . 32.8 inches (83.3 cm)

Sources: National Climatic Data Center, NESDIS, NOAA, U.S. Department of Commerce

In the Lower Peninsula, the average temperatures in July range from 64 to 83 degrees Fahrenheit (18 to 28 degrees Celsius). In January, the temperatures average 18° to 31°F (–8° to –1°C). Average annual snowfall is 30 to 40 inches (76 to 102 centimeters). Weather in the Upper Peninsula is harsher. The July temperatures range from 52° to 76°F (11° to 24°C). But the January average ranges from just 5° to 22°F (–15° to –6°C). And the snowfall? In some areas, it can total between 20 and 25 feet (6 and 8 m) a year! But Michiganians (or Michiganders) know how to make the most of it.

MINI-BIO

E. GENEVIEVE GILLETTE: PARK LOVER

E. Genevieve Gillette (1898–1986) was born in Lansing and attended the Michigan Agricultural College, which is now Michigan State University. In 1920, she was the only woman to graduate from the college's first landscape architecture program. Gillette loved the outdoors and wanted to conserve Michigan's wild areas for everyone to enjoy. Starting in 1924, she helped raise money for parks including Hartwick Pines State Park, Ludington State Park, Porcupine Mountains Wilderness State Park, Sleeping Bear Dunes National Lakeshore, and Pictured Rocks National Lakeshore. She also founded the Michigan Parks Association. No wonder she is called Miss Michigan State Parks.

Want to know more? See www.mecprotects.org/MER/fall06/gillette.htm

PLANT LIFE

Forests cover more than half of Michigan. And timber—the wood that is harvested from trees—is one of the state's greatest natural resources. There are many different kinds of trees: spruce, cedar, elm, ash, oak, hickory, beech, maple, and white pine, Michigan's state tree. Tasty fruit grows on apple and cherry trees there, too. It is estimated that there are 19.3 million acres (7.8 million hectares) of timber in Michigan, and more than 200,000 people make a living from these forests.

Pine cone

ANIMAL LIFE

Michigan's abundant water makes it ideal for fish and waterfowl. Swimming in the lakes are salmon, muskie, bass, perch, and catfish, as well as many other types of fish. The shores are home to egrets, great blue herons, gulls, terns, and loons, to name a few. A variety of animals live in the forests and near Michigan's water. There are bears, deer, squirrels, wolves, rabbits, and rac-

Michigan National Park Areas

This map shows some of Michigan's national parks, monuments, preserves, and other areas protected by the National Park Service.

ENDANGERED ANIMALS

Michigan's natural areas make the state a great place to live and visit. But as with other states, Michigan finds a number of its animals to be in danger. Some endangered animals are the eastern puma, the Indiana bat, and the gray wolf. Endangered birds include the Kirtland's warbler and the piping plover. Even insects, such as the American burying beetle, the Karner blue butterfly, and the Mitchell's satyr dragonfly, find their habitats to be threatened. What is Michigan doing about it? Its Department of Natural Resources created the Wildlife Action Plan, a program that calls for the preservation of habitats to help protect endangered species and to prevent other animals from ever becoming threatened.

Want to know more? See www.michigan.gov/dnr

coons—not to mention moose, which can weigh up to 1,000 pounds (450 kilograms) each. Bald eagles grace Michigan's skies, as do golden eagles, Canada geese, ospreys, and peregrine falcons.

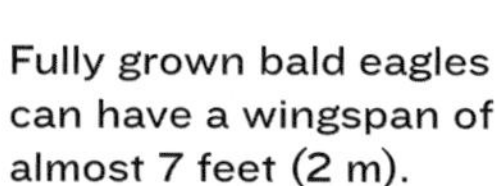
Fully grown bald eagles can have a wingspan of almost 7 feet (2 m).

SAVING RESOURCES

Michigan has acres and acres of forests. Their autumn colors are spectacular. And their timber is crucial to paper manufacturing and house building. So when fire threatens Michigan's forests, firefighters act quickly. In addition to dousing flames with water, they also construct **firebreaks** and drop special chemicals from planes to put out the fires. Michigan's Department of Natural Resources works to prevent fires and protect the land that Michiganians call home.

Some of Michigan's natural areas have been turned into housing developments and commercial areas.

WORD TO KNOW

firebreaks *barriers of cleared land created as a way to stop forest fires from spreading*

Q: DO TRUMPETER SWANS REALLY TRUMPET?

A: Well, actually, their honks do sound almost exactly like trumpets! It's a wonderful sound to hear in Michigan and throughout the Great Lakes region.

These changes have hurt some wild animals by damaging their environment and sometimes destroying their homes. Both government and nonprofit groups are trying to preserve some wild areas. The Nature Conservancy in Michigan teamed up with the U.S. Fish and Wildlife Service to double the size of the Detroit River International Wildlife Refuge and provide an even bigger space for Michigan animals to live.

At one point, the trumpeter swan was thought to be extinct in Michigan. But the birds—the largest waterfowl in the world—were reintroduced in the state. From 2000 to 2005, the population of trumpeter swans almost doubled, from 400 to 728.

Meanwhile, the Michigan Recycling Coalition works to reduce garbage by reusing and recycling. Michigan also led the way in banning nonreturnable beverage cans, with a pioneering law in 1976. Some

The trumpeter swan population has made a remarkable comeback in Michigan.

Volunteers from Redford Township clear logs and help clean up the Rouge River as part of an annual program called Rouge Rescue.

companies allow chemicals to run off into Michigan's beautiful waters. But the West Michigan Environmental Action Council has helped enact programs for keeping the lakes and rivers clean.

Michiganians have great spirit. When they see a problem, they work together to solve it. When it comes to protecting their state's resources, they show what teamwork is all about.

"The greatest reason for hope about Michigan's environmental future is that we have a populace that cares about our environmental future. Even residents who spend 100 percent of their time in a concrete, urban setting can respond to environmental values in this state because of a sense of place—that Michigan is special."

Dave Dempsey, author of *Ruin and Recovery: Michigan's Rise as a Conservation Leader*, 2001

READ ABOUT

The First Inhabitants....22

Native American Groups 22

Ways of Life.........25

A fisherman on the shore of Lake Superior beside Silver Cascade

c. 11,000 BCE
The first residents come to present-day Michigan

c. 4000 BCE
The Archaic people inhabit the region

▲ **c. 2500 BCE**
The Woodland culture begins

FIRST PEOPLE

★

ABOUT 30,000 YEARS AGO, PEOPLE FOLLOWED ELEPHANT-LIKE MASTODONS AND OTHER PREHISTORIC ANIMALS ACROSS A LAND BRIDGE THAT ONCE CONNECTED NORTHEAST ASIA TO THE NORTHWEST AMERICAS. Over thousands of years, these people spread throughout the Americas, and some of their descendants came to what is now Michigan.

c. 10 BCE
The Hopewell build their mounds

▲1600s
Europeans explore Michigan

1881 ►
Sanilac Petroglyphs are discovered at Bad Axe

SEE IT HERE!

EXHIBIT MUSEUM OF NATURAL HISTORY

If you'd like to learn about life in Michigan long ago, the Exhibit Museum of Natural History at the University of Michigan has lots to show you. There you'll find displays about prehistoric life, Michigan wildlife, and Native American cultures. In the Hall of Evolution, there are partial or complete skeletons of nine dinosaurs—the most extensive dinosaur exhibit in Michigan. About 20,000 students visit the museum each year. Want to know more? See www.lsa.umich.edu/exhibitmuseum

THE FIRST INHABITANTS

The first people to set foot in what is now Michigan probably arrived around 11,000 BCE, as the glaciers retreated and melting ice formed the Great Lakes. They most likely moved in and out of the region, hunting caribou and other large animals with stone-tipped spears.

About 7,000 years later, the Archaic people came to the area. They had learned to make tools and other objects from copper, which they mined near Lake Superior. Thousands of years passed, and next came the Woodland culture, which began in about 2500 BCE. This culture evolved into the ancestors of modern Michigan's Ojibwa (Chippewa), Odawa (Ottawa), Potawatomi, Huron (Wyandot), Menominee, Fox, Sauk (Sac), Miami, and Winnebago (or Ho-Chunk) groups.

NATIVE AMERICAN GROUPS

In prehistoric times, the largest of Michigan's many Native American groups was the Huron. They lived in the area near Lakes Ontario, Erie, and Huron. They relied heavily on the crops they farmed—corn, squash, and beans. But they also fished and hunted bison, bear, and deer. This group settled in villages and usually stayed put. They did not move around like other groups sometimes did.

Fishing in a birchbark canoe in Lake Michigan

Native American Peoples

(Before European Contact)

This map shows the general area of Native American peoples before European settlers arrived.

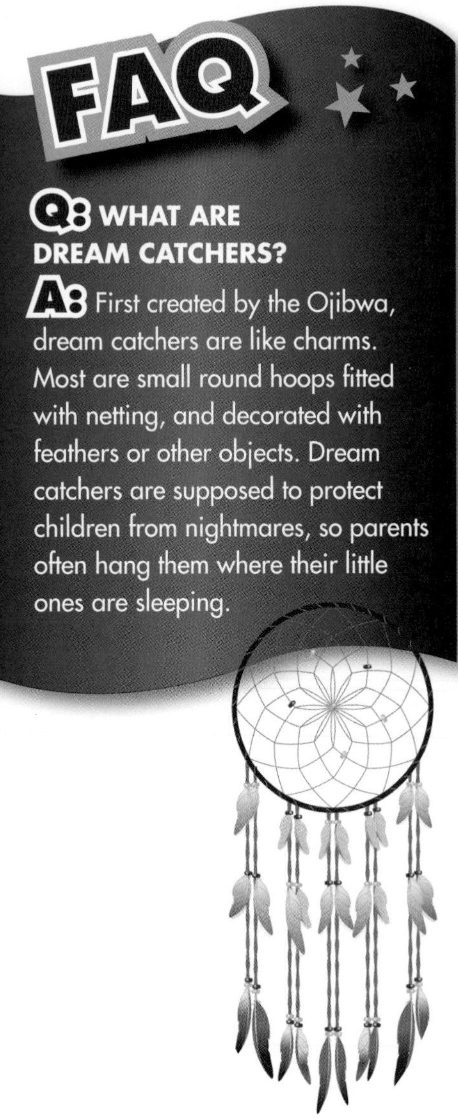

Q: WHAT ARE DREAM CATCHERS?

A: First created by the Ojibwa, dream catchers are like charms. Most are small round hoops fitted with netting, and decorated with feathers or other objects. Dream catchers are supposed to protect children from nightmares, so parents often hang them where their little ones are sleeping.

Three Native American groups—the Ojibwa, the Odawa, and the Potawatomi—formed the Council of Three Fires. The relationship helped the three groups work together to survive. The Ojibwa lived along the southern shore of Lake Superior. They were skilled hunters and fishers and had unique methods for harvesting wild rice and extracting sugar from maple trees. They are known for their beautiful dream catchers. The Odawa traded with other groups. The Ojibwa also made fine canoes from bark. Because many of the Odawa lived along Lake Michigan, this method of transportation helped them in their trading activities. The Potawatomi were great farmers and grew melons, beans, squash, corn, and tobacco. They lived in what is now southern Michigan.

The Hopewell built elaborate burial mounds. The mounds, built between 10 BCE and 400 CE, are hills of stone or earth where the dead were buried. The Hopewell made weapons, tools, and religious objects from copper and other raw materials. Sometimes they put these items in the burial mounds with the dead. Today, you can see some of these burial mounds in Grand Rapids.

The Sanilac Petroglyphs were discovered in Bad Axe, near the Cass River, in 1881. These sandstone carvings show images of panthers, deer, and a Native American archer. They date back as far as 1,000 years ago.

The Hopewell built mounds that were used as burial places.

Native American wigwam at the historic Colonial Fort Michilimackinac, in Mackinaw City

MINI-BIO

LOIS BEARDSLEE: ARTIST AND STORYTELLER

The Sisters of the Great Lakes is a group of women who celebrate their ancient Native American traditions through art. Lois Beardslee (1976–) is an Ojibwa who lives in Maple City. She uses paint made from pigments she finds in northern Michigan, and she also makes beautiful items with beads. Beardslee creates traditional Ojibwa cut-out decorations from pieces of birch bark strips. She is one of only two people who still practice this art. In addition, Beardslee is a talented storyteller, and *Lies to Live By* is a collection of her tales.

Want to know more? See museum.msu.edu/museum/tes/sisters/beardslee.htm

WAYS OF LIFE

Native Americans in Michigan often lived in dome-shaped wigwams, which were shelters they built from young trees, animal hides, and bark.

In most villages, the women and girls did the cooking, planting, and harvesting. They wove nets for fishing, and they turned animal hides into leather. The men and boys made canoes and wigwams, as well as traps and bows and arrows for hunting.

Most of the early groups were peaceful. They seldom fought with other groups. When they did, it was usually because one group had moved too close to the other. In general, people believed that the land, animals, and plants belonged to everyone. They believed no one could control another person. And they believed that spirits were more powerful than humans. But their nonviolent way of life would never be the same after European explorers arrived in the 1600s.

READ ABOUT

Missionaries and Explorers 28

The Mighty Fur Trade 28

Competing for Control. 31

Pontiac's Rebellion 32

The American Revolution 32

The Northwest Territory 33

Explorer Jean Nicolet lands on the shore of Lake Michigan in 1634.

1618

Étienne Brûlé reaches Sault Sainte Marie

1668 ►

Jacques Marquette founds the first permanent European settlement in Michigan

1701

Antoine de la Mothe, Sieur de Cadillac, establishes Fort Pontchartrain

EXPLORATION AND SETTLEMENT

★

FRENCH EXPLORERS WERE LOOKING FOR A ROUTE TO CHINA WHEN THEY STUMBLED ON THE GREAT LAKES. When they arrived in what is now Michigan, they found forests teeming with wildlife. And they encountered Native Americans who had called this land home for many generations. Rather than continue looking for a route to China, many of these explorers decided to stay. The lives of both groups would be changed forever.

1763
Pontiac's Rebellion takes place

1783
The Treaty of Paris is signed

1796
The U.S. flag is raised over Detroit

Samuel de Champlain, early 1600s

MISSIONARIES AND EXPLORERS

Michigan's earliest European explorers came mostly from France. In the early 1600s, Samuel de Champlain was governor of New France (now known as Canada). He sent one of his men, Étienne Brûlé, through the Georgian Bay and Lake Huron. Brûlé reached the Sault Sainte Marie area in 1618. In 1621, he traveled as far west as the Keweenaw Peninsula. He was probably the first European to arrive in Michigan.

In the 1630s, Jean Nicolet explored the Lake Michigan region. When he reached Green Bay, Wisconsin, he thought he had landed in China. He was mistaken.

In 1660, René Ménard started a **mission** on Keweenaw Bay, on the Upper Peninsula. He was a Catholic missionary who hoped to **convert** the Native Americans to Christianity. However, Indians had their own spiritual traditions, and few were interested in changing them.

Eight years later, Father Jacques Marquette founded the first permanent European settlement in Michigan, in Sault Sainte Marie. By the early 1700s, the French built a military post at Mackinaw City (Fort Michilimackinac) to protect the fur traders and missionaries.

WORDS TO KNOW

mission *a place created by a religious group to spread its beliefs*

convert *to bring a person over from one opinion or belief to another*

THE MIGHTY FUR TRADE

Other French people came to Michigan to take advantage of its plentiful wildlife. With Michigan's Native Americans, the French built a great fur-trading system. Fashion was very important in France, and fur was in high demand. There weren't enough animals in France to satisfy the need. So the French were quick to exploit North America's populations of mink, beavers, foxes, and other animals.

Exploration of Michigan

The colored arrows on this map show the routes taken by explorers between 1620 and 1634.

MINI-BIO

JACQUES MARQUETTE: MISSIONARY AND EXPLORER

He may have spent just nine years in North America, but the Jesuit missionary Jacques Marquette (1637–1675) left a big mark. Marquette was born in France and traveled to present-day Michigan in hopes of bringing Christianity to the Native Americans. He founded missions at Sault Sainte Marie and the Straits of Mackinac. In 1673, he and Louis Jolliet, a French Canadian, joined six other men to explore the Mississippi River. They became the first Europeans to set their eyes on the great river. Marquette became ill during this journey and died at the age of 39. The city of Marquette is named after him.

Want to know more? See www.biographi.ca/EN/ShowBio.asp?BioID-34519&query=marquette

Native Americans profited from the French desire for furs. They trapped the prized animals and traded their furs for guns, axes, cloth, and other materials. Before long, the fur-bearing animals were so widely hunted that they began disappearing from the region. So the trappers and traders moved farther west, in search of these valuable creatures. A group of French Canadians called voyageurs paddled their canoes—sometimes up to 18 hours a day—to retrieve bundles of furs to sell in Montreal. They told wonderful stories through the songs they sang and had great physical strength.

One French explorer, René-Robert Cavelier, Sieur de La Salle, was also a keen businessman. To expand his fur trade, he set up forts between the Great Lakes and the Mississippi River. In 1701, Antone de la Mothe Cadillac established Fort Pontchartrain, which became a center for fur trading, as well as a site for farming. This spot eventually became the city of Detroit. (The name Detroit comes from the French word for "strait," which is pronounced "DET-wa.") Another fur-trading hub was located at the Straits of Mackinac.

COMPETING FOR CONTROL

As the French grew wealthier from the fur trade, the British wanted a part of the action. They had set up colonies along what is now the East Coast of the United States, and they became interested in the land farther west. This led to conflict between the French and the British. The French tried to strengthen their hold on the region by forming an **alliance** with various Native American groups. But even that partnership did not save the French. They were soon battling British troops in the French and Indian War (1754–1763).

Under the leadership of Major Robert Rogers, the British gained control of the fort at Detroit on November 29, 1760. They took over the other French posts the following year. Like the French, the British were most interested in the furs from this region. They didn't plan to settle there or disrupt the Native Americans' way of life. However, the Native people had become friendly with the French. Many disliked the British, whose trading practices were often unfair. And little by little, British colonists were beginning to move into nearby western Pennsylvania and the Ohio region. This movement forced many Native Americans off their lands.

WORD TO KNOW

alliance *an association between groups that benefits all the members*

Trappers on a lake waiting to snare their prey

WORDS TO KNOW

siege *a military blockade (the closing down of a city or fort to outside people and supplies), usually used to make a group surrender*

treaty *an agreement between two or more groups, often to end a conflict*

PONTIAC'S REBELLION

In the spring of 1763, Odawa chief Pontiac led a group of Native Americans who rose up against the British. They attacked British posts from Pennsylvania to Lake Superior. Pontiac's forces captured many forts. His forces, white colonists reported, killed whites, and embraced enslaved Africans as friends and allies.

Pontiac led an attack on the fort at Detroit. He and his men failed to take the fort, but they kept it under **siege** for seven months. Then Pontiac learned that France had signed a **treaty** with Great Britain, surrendering the entire region. Realizing he would get no help from the French, he finally withdrew from Detroit.

MINI-BIO

PONTIAC: REBEL LEADER

Some say Pontiac (c. 1720–1769) was an Odawa chief. Others say that he was only a respected leader. Some say that Pontiac orchestrated the entire battle known as Pontiac's Rebellion. Others say he just took part. Whatever the true story is, Pontiac tried to prevent British control of Native American land. His efforts to drive the British out of the fort at Detroit failed. But his leadership inspired his people. Pontiac died in Illinois after being attacked by a Peoria Indian. He is supposedly buried on Apple Island, near Pontiac, the Michigan city named after him.

Want to know more? See www.biographi.ca/EN/ShowBio.asp?BioId=35719

THE AMERICAN REVOLUTION

As the British hold on the region increased, they were concerned about preserving the forests that were home to the fur-bearing animals. So they tried to prevent anyone from settling on the land. When the American Revolution (1775–1783) began, the Michigan wilderness was still populated by Native Americans.

Though this region saw no real fighting during the Revolution, the British used Detroit as a central post. From there, they sent out soldiers to battle the American soldiers.

In 1781, the British also fended off an attack from the Spanish. Spanish forces captured Fort St. Joseph in present-day Niles. But they controlled the fort for only one day before the British took it back.

By 1782, the American colonists had shown their determination and strength. The British were ready to make peace. The following year, American and British leaders signed the Treaty of Paris, which ended the war. In their agreement, a line that stretched through the middle of the Great Lakes and their connecting rivers became the official boundary between Canada and the United States.

THE NORTHWEST TERRITORY

Though the British agreed to give up their posts in Michigan, they were in no hurry. They remained in the region, with their flag flying over Detroit. In fact, it took 13 years for the British to finally leave. On August 20, 1794, General "Mad Anthony" Wayne led U.S. troops in the Battle of Fallen Timbers near present-day Toledo, Ohio. This conflict forced the Native Americans out of the area and weakened the British position. About two years later, the British troops traveled north into Canada, and on July 11, 1796, the U.S. flag was finally raised over Detroit.

The Northwest Ordinance of 1787 set up a system of government for the territories taken from the British after the Revolution, and it banned slavery from these territories. After the Revolution, Michigan became part of the Northwest Territory. This region included what are now Ohio, Indiana, Illinois, Wisconsin, Michigan, and parts of Minnesota. It wouldn't be long before Michigan became a state.

WOW

These days, the City of Niles has a special claim to fame: it's the only place in Michigan to have had flags from four different countries—France, Great Britain, Spain, and the United States—flying over it!

Fort Mackinac

READ ABOUT

The Michigan Territory 36

The War of 1812 38

Settling in Michigan 39

Becoming a State 41

Facing Civil War 45

The New Century 48

By 1800, the city of Detroit was becoming a bustling port city.

1813
The Battle of River Raisin is fought

▲1825
The Erie Canal opens

▲1837
Michigan becomes a state

GROWTH AND CHANGE

★

MICHIGAN WAS CHANGING EARLY IN THE 19TH CENTURY. In 1800, the western part of the Northwest Territory became the Territory of Indiana, including part of Michigan's Lower Peninsula. Ohio became a state in 1803, and all of today's Michigan became part of the Indiana Territory.

1852
Michigan's first labor union is formed

▲ **1908**
Henry Ford introduces the Model T

1917–1918
About 135,000 Michiganians join the military during World War I

THE MICHIGAN TERRITORY

On January 11, 1805, Michigan's future was set in motion. President Thomas Jefferson signed a document that created the Michigan Territory, with Detroit as its capital.

When Michigan became a separate territory, about 4,000 white settlers were living there. Most of them had made homes at Detroit, Mackinac Island, River Raisin, and Sault Sainte Marie. The territory included all of the Lower Peninsula and the eastern tip of the present Upper Peninsula. At that time, the southern border was marked by a line drawn straight east through the southernmost tip of Lake Michigan.

That same year, President Jefferson appointed William Hull to be the first governor of Michigan Territory. Born in Connecticut, he had served as a general in the American Revolution. The territory's first government included Hull, a secretary, and three judges. Only one of these five men had been living in Michigan. Just before the five took office, fire destroyed Detroit. One of the appointed judges, Augustus B. Woodward, drew up plans for rebuilding the town. He based his plans on the model of Washington, D.C., but they were never fully carried out.

A view of Detroit in 1815

Michigan: From Territory to Statehood

(1805–1837)

This map shows the original Michigan territory and the area (outlined in red) that became the state of Michigan in 1837.

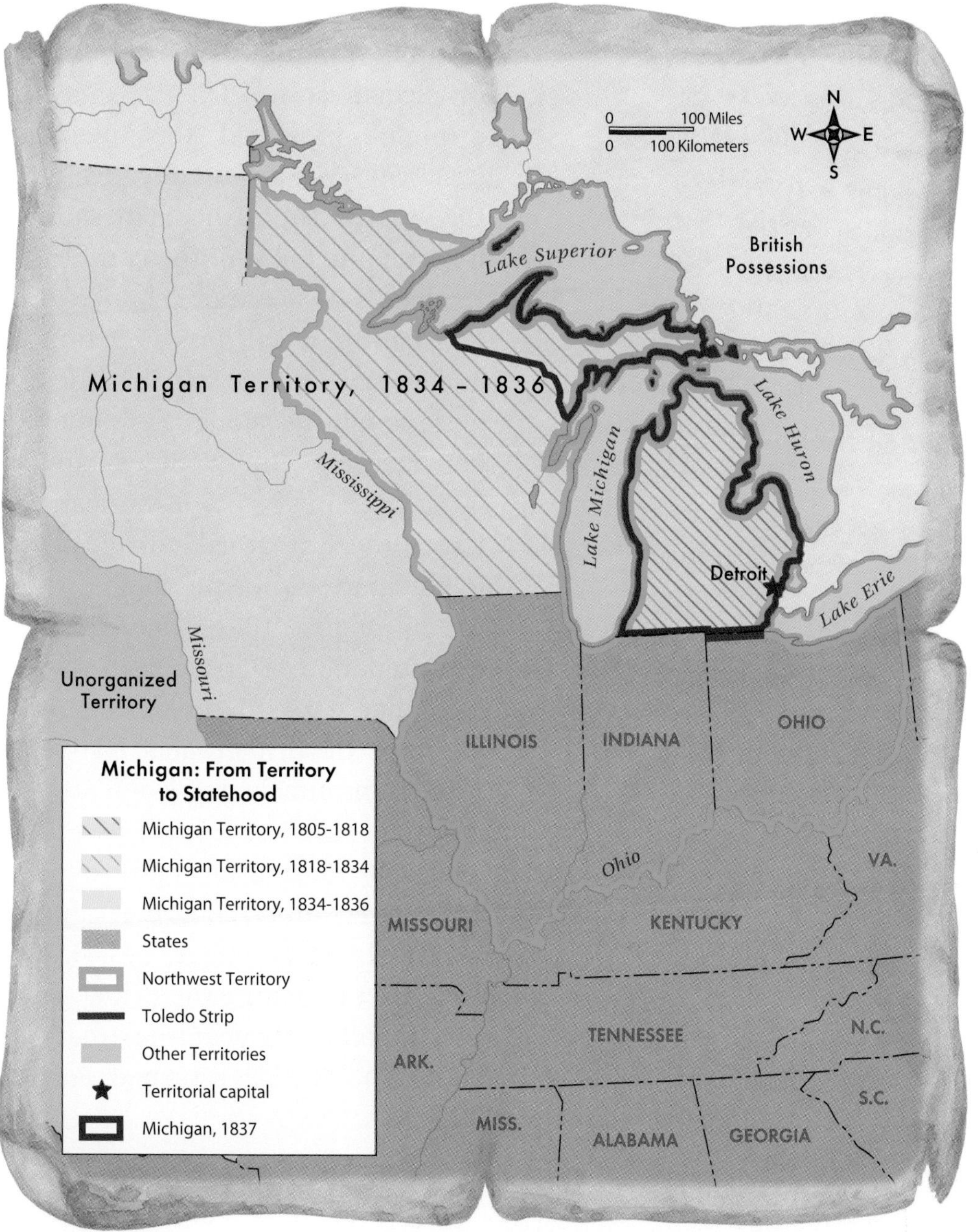

MINI-BIO

TECUMSEH: DEFENDER OF HIS PEOPLE

After the Battle of Fallen Timbers, many Ohio Indians thought the best way to survive the settlers was to give in to them. Shawnee leader Tecumseh (c. 1768–1813) disagreed and urged his people to defend themselves. During the War of 1812, Tecumseh fought alongside the British and helped them take Detroit. However, this success was short-lived. During the Battle of the Thames, near Chatham, Ontario, a combined force of British and Native Americans fought U.S. troops led by William Henry Harrison. At one point, the British fled the battlefield, leaving the Native Americans on their own. Sometime during the skirmish with the American troops, a bullet hit Tecumseh, killing him. His hopes of preserving Native American land died along with him.

Want to know more? See www.ohiohistorycentral.org/entry.php?rec=373

THE WAR OF 1812

The Americans had gained independence from Great Britain, but their troubles with the British were hardly over. British forces had begun capturing U.S. sailors and forcing them to work on British ships. The U.S. government protested this illegal practice. That eventually led to the War of 1812. Michigan soon became one focus of the conflict. England saw one more chance to gain control of the forts at Detroit and on Mackinac Island. So battles were fought all along the border between the United States and Canada. Many Native Americans joined the British in their efforts to defeat the American forces.

In August 1812, the British captured both Detroit and Fort Mackinac. In January 1813, a group of British and Native Americans attacked and defeated U.S. troops near present-day Monroe. Known as the Battle of River Raisin, it was the most deadly battle ever fought in Michigan. During the conflict, 280 Americans and 24 British men were killed. In September 1813, U.S. soldiers took back Detroit after defeating the British at the Battle of Lake Erie. The following year, the Treaty of Ghent ended the war. The British returned Fort Mackinac to the United States.

American and British battleships exchange fire on the waters of Lake Erie in 1813, in one of the many battles over who controlled the Great Lakes.

SETTLING IN MICHIGAN

After the War of 1812, people were slow to move to Michigan. Some settlers believed it was not suitable for farming. Many chose instead to make their homes in Illinois and Missouri. Also, for several years it was unclear what land the U.S. government had granted to the Native Americans and what was available for settlements.

In the 1820s, Lewis Cass, governor of the territory, tried to change Michigan's image. He convinced the U.S. government to build roads and lighthouses, so people could travel more easily.

WORD TO KNOW

mediator *someone who helps others settle their differences*

MINI-BIO

HENRY SCHOOLCRAFT: INDIAN AGENT

What was an Indian agent? That was the title Henry Schoolcraft (1793–1864) was given when he went to Sault Sainte Marie in 1822. His job was to get to know the Native Americans and serve as a **mediator** between them and the U.S. government. He learned the Ojibwa language from his wife, Jane Johnston, the daughter of an Irish fur trader and an Ojibwa woman. He wrote down his observations of the Native people and helped others understand the Indians. His writings inspired Henry Wadsworth Longfellow to compose his poem "The Song of Hiawatha." Schoolcraft College in Livonia is named in his honor, as are the village of Schoolcraft and Schoolcraft County in Michigan.

Want to know more? See www.schoolcraft.edu/archives/henry_rowe_schoolcraft.asp

Picture Yourself . . .

at the Mt. Pleasant School

If you were a Native American child in the late 1800s, you might have had to attend the Mt. Pleasant School. But there was nothing pleasant about this school. As a student here, you'd have to wear military-like uniforms and live in dormitories with other boys and girls. School officials would cut your hair short and teach you "white man's ways." You could speak only English. If you lapsed into your native language, someone would wash your mouth out with soap. If you disobeyed the rules, someone might beat you with a strap or a rubber hose. And if you just couldn't stand it, you might run away. If you still lived in the region in 1933, you would be happy to see the school close!

He negotiated land treaties with the Native Americans. After these treaties were signed (1819–1821), more land opened up for settlers. So more and more people from the eastern United States came to the Michigan Territory. New roads were built into the central part of the region. And for the first time, the U.S. government sponsored public sales of land.

In 1825, laborers finished building on a 363-mile (584-km) waterway through New York State that linked the Atlantic Ocean with the Great Lakes. Suddenly, there was a cheap way to get to the western territories, and it was called the Erie Canal. A large number of farmers from New England and New York came to Michigan Territory by way of the canal. The territory grew faster than any other part of the United States. In 1820, Michigan had almost 9,000 settlers. Just ten years later, that number had grown to nearly 32,000.

The Erie Canal has been essential to Michigan's economy and transportation system since its opening in 1825.

Michigan's first election was held in 1837.

In 1840, the population had reached more than 200,000. As settlers poured into Michigan, the population doubled by 1850 and again by 1860. It wasn't long before farming became more important than fur trading in this region.

As new settlers moved in and built towns, the original settlers, Native Americans, were forced off their land. Slowly, more and more land treaties were signed, and the Native Americans soon were moved onto reservations, putting an end to traditional Indian life.

SEE IT HERE!

LOOKOUT POINT

If you can't imagine what life was like in the Michigan Territory, visit Fort Wilkins and Copper Harbor Lighthouse. The fort was built in 1844 as a U.S. Army post, and its soldiers were supposed to maintain peace in the copper country. Today, there are 19 restored buildings. Tour guides in 19th-century costumes are happy to answer your questions. Also on-site is the Copper Harbor Lighthouse, which dates back to 1848. And what a view!

BECOMING A STATE

The settlers who came to Michigan were from a variety of backgrounds. In general, New Englanders and New Yorkers settled the southern areas of the state, Dutch farmers settled in the southwest, and Germans favored the Saginaw Valley. Many people of Irish descent settled in the southeast, while Finns and Italians moved into the Upper Peninsula.

Michigan was on its way to being a state. The people organized a state government in 1835 and asked to join the Union—but there was one delay. Ohio and Michigan were fighting over who owned the region near the city of

Q: WHY IS MICHIGAN SOMETIMES CALLED THE WOLVERINE STATE?

A: Good question, since it appears that the wolverine—a large weasel—never even lived in the state. Some say it's a reference to the 1835 Toledo War. Apparently, wolverines are supposed to be ornery creatures. So Ohioans called the Michiganians "wolverines" as the two sides argued over the Toledo Strip. Years later, the University of Michigan adopted the wolverine as its mascot.

Toledo, especially the area at the mouth of the Maumee River. When Ohio claimed to own this "Toledo Strip," Michigan sent armed men to the region. But the Toledo War was a short one, and only one man was hurt. In the end, the U.S. Congress convinced Michigan to give up the Toledo Strip.

On January 26, 1837, Michigan became the 26th state. The first governor was Stevens T. Mason, who was just 24 years old when he was elected. He had succeeded Lewis Cass, who had been governor of the Michigan Territory. Mason encouraged the founding of state-supported schools. And he led efforts to locate the University of Michigan in the town of Ann Arbor. He left office in 1840 and still holds the record for being the state's youngest governor.

Since Michigan's statehood, Detroit had been its capital. But in 1847, the capital moved to the more centrally located city of Lansing. Workers laid rail lines and built new roads. The Wolverine State was booming.

Picture Yourself . . .

as a Michigan pioneer

First, you and your family traveled into this wilderness with nothing but a horse-drawn wagon to carry all your possessions. The trail was rough, and often the wagon got stuck. If you had to cross a river or stream, you got really wet—because there were no bridges yet. When you arrived in Michigan, you would have to build a log cabin on the land your parents had bought. You would help cut down trees and bring 50 to 60 logs to the site. Then you would work to make these logs into a one-room home. You would cut out some windows and a door. But since you had no glass, your windows would be made of greased paper.

Finally, you and your family would clear the land and plant crops. Whatever you didn't eat or store to eat later, you would sell to others. You might have some livestock, too. But wild animals could destroy your crops and kill your livestock. And you were at the mercy of the weather. Too little rain or too much wind meant your crops would die. The odds were against you. But you and your family would fight the odds to survive.

THE UNDERGROUND RAILROAD

As Michigan was growing, the United States was facing a complicated problem: slavery. Throughout the South, plantation owners depended on slaves to work the land. Enslaved people labored under grueling conditions. They were not paid for their work, they had no rights, and they were not allowed to leave. Many Northern states opposed this practice. Michigan was a Free State, meaning it did not allow slavery. Some runaways who reached Michigan were able to win their liberty in state courts. Others managed to escape posses and find freedom. Still others were aided by Michigan residents who were ready to attack posses if necessary to rescue **fugitives**.

The Underground Railroad was a series of hiding places for slaves who escaped their masters. The slaves left the South and traveled through the North on their way to freedom in Canada. Many of the "stations" on the railroad were Michigan homes, barns, schools, and

WORD TO KNOW

fugitives *people who flee or try to escape*

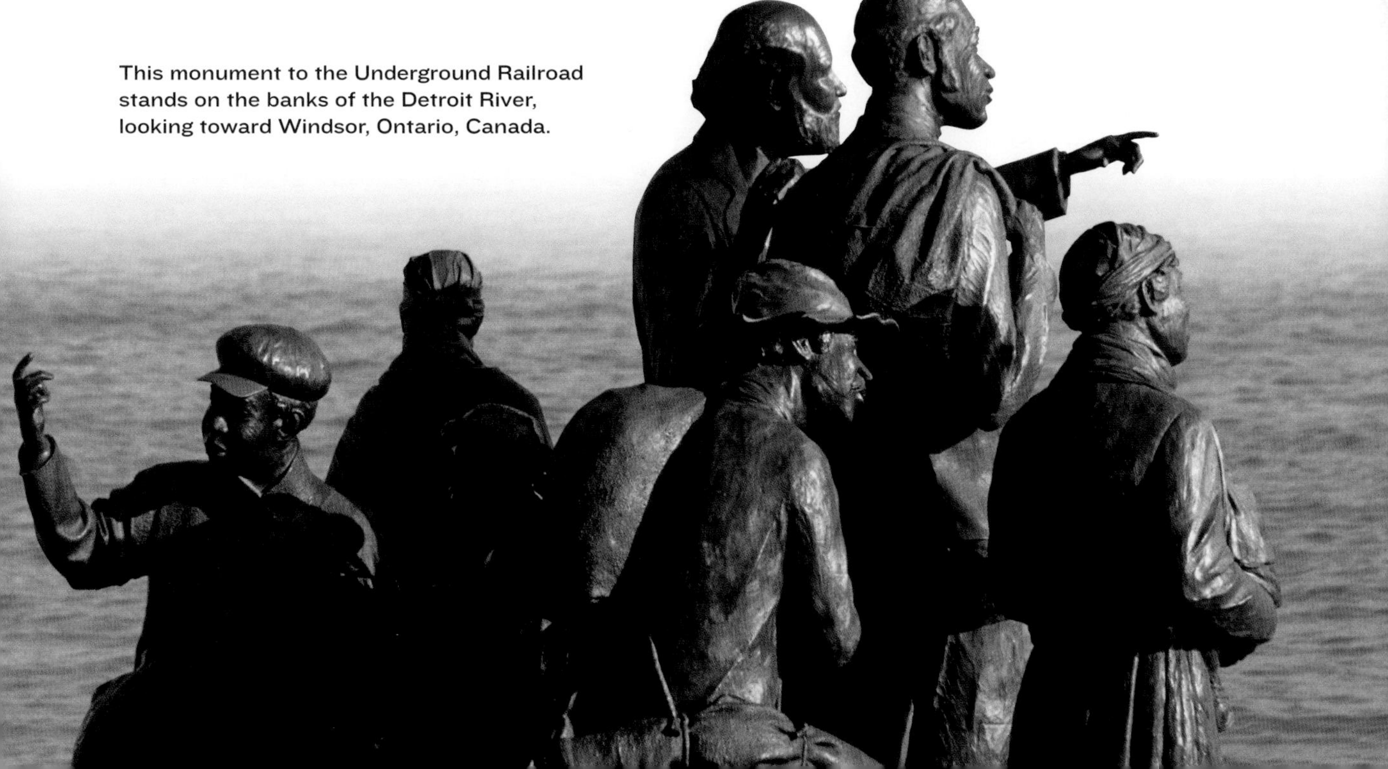

This monument to the Underground Railroad stands on the banks of the Detroit River, looking toward Windsor, Ontario, Canada.

stores. In 1832, Laura Haviland and Elizabeth Chandler, two white women in Michigan formed the Female Anti-Slavery Society. They wanted to make sure as many fugitives as possible reached Canada. Haviland once said: "Let the slaveholder come and try us. . . . Let them disturb an escaped slave, at any time of the night or day, and the sound of tin horn would be heard, with a dozen or more answering it in different directions, and men enough would gather around the trembling fugitive for his rescue. For women can blow horns, and men can run."

In the 1840s, two young black men took over the Detroit station of the Underground Railroad. William Lambert and George DeBaptiste recruited only the most brave and trustworthy African Americans, and at least one white man, to liberate captured runaways. "It was fight and run—danger at every turn," recalled Lambert, "but that we calculated upon, and were prepared for." Lambert and DeBaptiste were successful businessmen who struggled for equality and education for African Americans. They helped organize statewide protests of Michigan's "Black Laws," which denied people of color the right to vote, to serve on juries, or to testify in court against white people.

The Second Baptist Church in Detroit dates to 1836 and was an important stop on the Underground Railroad.

FACING CIVIL WAR

The North wanted to outlaw slavery, while the South claimed it needed slaves to survive economically. Without slave labor, plantation owners' profits would suffer. In 1861, the Civil War erupted between the Union (the North) and the Confederacy (the South).

About 90,000 Michiganians fought for the Union during the Civil War. That included approximately 1,500 African Americans who served in the First Michigan Colored Infantry, formed in 1864. Some of these soldiers were recruited by Lambert and DeBaptiste.

These brave troops were proud to play a part in winning the war and ultimately ending slavery. After much loss

MICHIGAN WOMEN IN THE CIVIL WAR

During the Civil War, many women managed farms and businesses while their husbands and fathers joined the Union army. But some women saw the war up close.

One was **Annie Etheridge** (1839–1913) of Detroit, who served as a medic in the Union army. She tended to the wounded right on the battlefield. She kept her cool even as shots rang out around her. And she comforted the soldiers who needed her help.

Another was **Sarah E. Edmonds** (1842–1898) of Flint. She cut her hair, dressed in men's clothing, and called herself Frank Thompson because she wanted to be a soldier. She enlisted in the Michigan infantry and for two years served as a nurse and a spy. Sometimes when she spied on the Confederate troops, she wore disguises. Edmonds had to leave the army when she caught malaria. She feared her identity would be revealed during her medical treatment.

During the Civil War, Sarah E. Edmonds disguised herself as a man and served in the Michigan infantry.

A memorial to Michigan Civil War soldiers who fought in the Battle of Shiloh

of life and property, the fighting stopped when the Confederacy surrendered in 1865.

MAKING A LIVING

In the second half of the 18th century, people around the world saw the United States as the place to be. Industry was growing, and there was so much land to be had. Between 1860 and 1890, more than 700,000 immigrants decided to make Michigan their home. Most of these newcomers were from Europe and Canada.

Life in Michigan was demanding. There were lots of jobs, but the work was hard. Most industrial jobs involved long hours, little pay, and sometimes health hazards. Michiganians toiled in factories and mines, logged timber in the forests, and worked on farms.

Soon labor unions formed to help protect the rights of workers. They fought for better hours and higher pay, as well as safer factories. The oldest in Michigan is the International Typographical Union, which was founded in 1852. Other groups were created to protect stonecutters, blacksmiths, shoemakers, and many others. The efforts of these groups led to a shorter workday—8

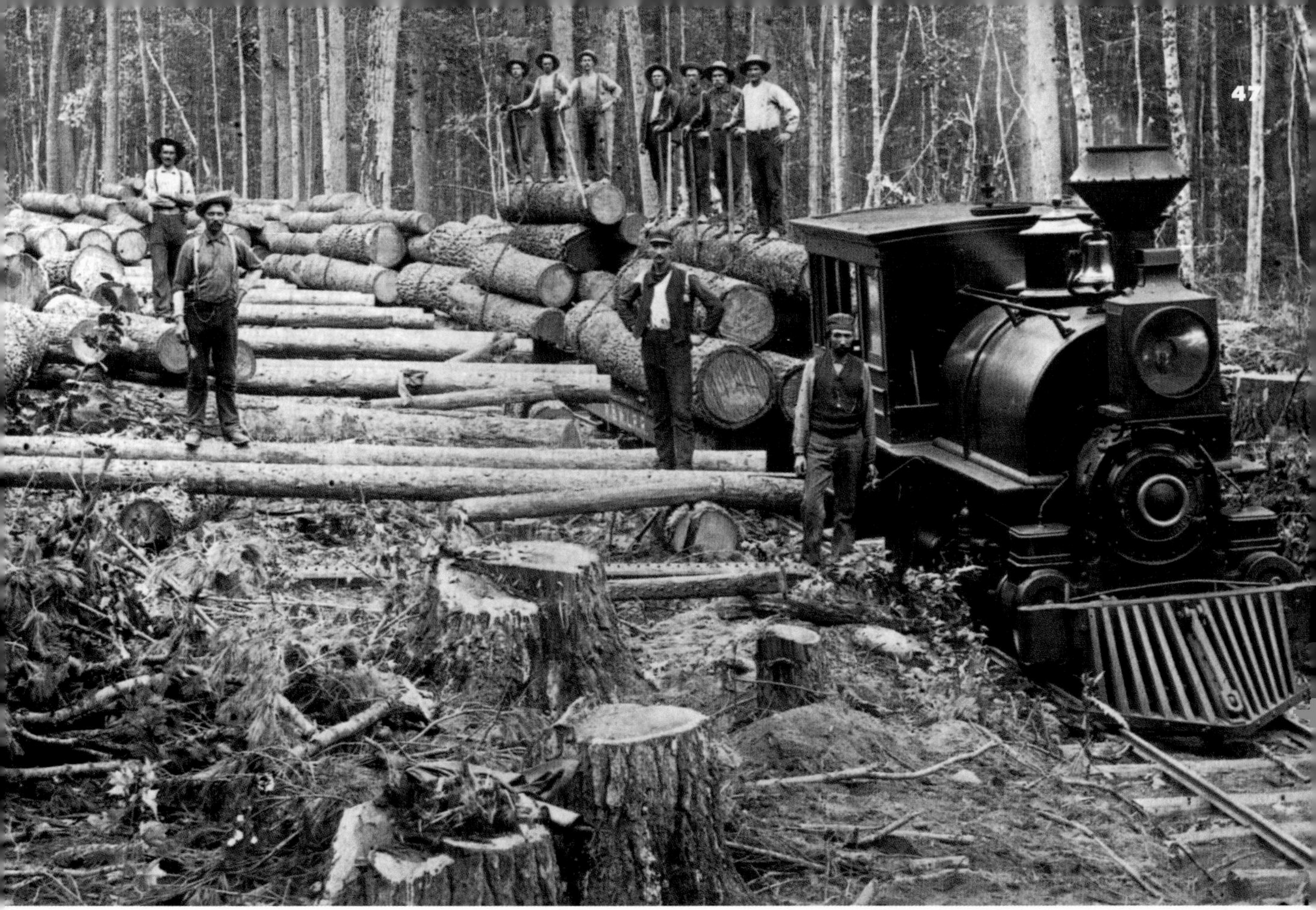

Logging was one of the many jobs that people could find in Michigan, but it was physically demanding work with low pay and long hours.

hours instead of 10 or 12. They also tried to improve the working conditions in factories and other businesses.

THE NEW CENTURY

As the 20th century began, the population of the state had reached almost 2.5 million people. And something huge was about to happen. In 1908, Henry Ford introduced the Model T automobile. Within the next few years, Ford developed assembly lines for automobile manufacturing. He and other innovators such as Ransom Olds, William C. Durant, and Walter Chrysler were about to change Michigan and the world.

But across the Atlantic, trouble was brewing. In 1917, the United States entered World War I (1914–1918). During the war, more than 135,000 Michiganians joined

FAQ

Q: WHAT DO LABOR UNIONS DO?

A: Labor unions represent workers and help protect their rights. They negotiate hours, wages, and other working conditions with employers.

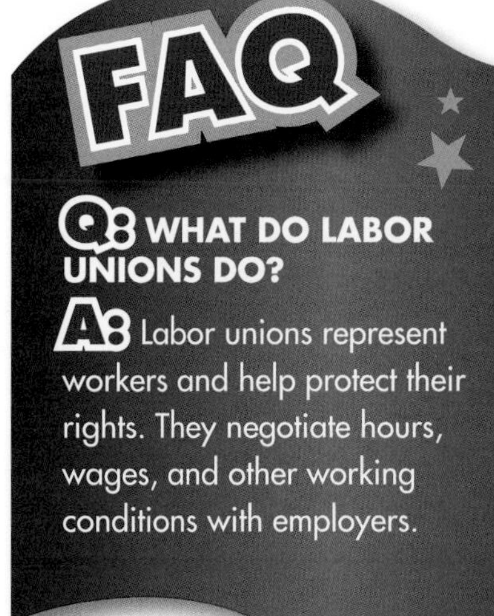

Auto workers lower the body of a Model T onto an assembly line ramp at the Ford Motor Company in Highland Park in 1914.

the armed forces, and nearly 13,000 died. Michigan also contributed to the war effort by producing supplies for the military. This manufacturing surge helped win the war and boosted growth in the state.

After the war, construction shot up in Michigan. Detroit erected many of its biggest buildings during this time: the General Motors Building, the Guardian

Building, and the Fisher Building, just to name a few. Meanwhile, that newfangled contraption—the car—was catching on. Automobile manufacturing created a huge number of jobs. People looking for work flocked to Michigan from Canada, Europe, and the South. The population of Flint increased from 13,000 to more than 156,000. Between 1900 and 1930, the population of Detroit grew from about 286,000 to nearly 1,600,000; Los Angeles was the only U.S. city that grew faster during that time. Michigan's future held great promise.

Several thousand factory workers and employees gather outside of the Ford Motor Company building in Detroit.

READ ABOUT

Facing Hardship 52

Gaining Ground. 53

Heading North 54

The Boom Years 55

Trying Times. 56

Looking Forward 59

Workers on a Ford Motor Company assembly line in 1930

1932
Ford's River Rouge Plant protest march turns violent

1941–1945
Michiganians fight in World War II

1957 ▲
The Mackinac Bridge opens

MORE MODERN TIMES

★

DETROIT'S SKYLINE WAS GROWING. The auto industry was taking the world by storm. With plenty of jobs available, people from all over decided to make Michigan their home. The 20th century began as a promising, bustling time for the Great Lakes State. But prosperity came to a slow skid during the Great Depression. Businesses closed and banks collapsed. Thousands of Michiganians lost their jobs and savings.

1963
Martin Luther King Jr. leads the Great March to Freedom

1980s
Michigan endures a recession

2001
Detroit celebrates its 300th anniversary

Men waiting in a soup line in Detroit during the Great Depression

The Michigan CCC planted 484 million trees, constructed 7,000 miles (11,000 km) of truck rails, and built 504 bridges and 222 buildings.

FACING HARDSHIP

The Depression was particularly hard on a state such as Michigan, which relied so heavily on industry. The automobile market was severely damaged as people hardly had money to buy food, never mind cars. For example, the Ford Motor Company had 128,000 workers in 1929. By 1931, it had just 37,000. Michiganians hoped the federal government would help out.

On March 7, 1932, violence broke out at Ford's River Rouge Plant in Dearborn. A peaceful group of 3,000 marchers protested that not enough people were employed at the plant. But the gathering was broken up by security guards and police who used guns, tear gas, and water hoses on the marchers. Five marchers died, and 60 were wounded in the confrontation.

MINI-BIO

WALTER REUTHER: LABOR LEADER

While the auto industry grew in Michigan, Walter Reuther (1907–1970) became one of many people concerned for the workers' welfare. On January 11, 1937, he and his brothers, Victor and Roy, organized a **sit-down strike** at a GM plant in Flint. This inspired other workers to do the same at auto plants throughout the state. On May 26, 1937, Reuther and other United Auto Workers members were handing out literature at a Ford auto plant when Ford security guards attacked them. Reuther was among those brutally beaten. This incident became known as the Battle of the Overpass. Now Reuther was even more determined to continue his union work. He served as president of the United Auto Workers from 1946 until he died. Thanks to him, the workers' voices were always heard.

Want to know more? See www.reuther.wayne.edu/exhibits/wpr.html

GAINING GROUND

After his election in 1932, President Franklin Delano Roosevelt created social programs that helped get people back on their feet. One program was the Civilian Conservation Corps (CCC). This group recruited the unemployed to work at jobs that protected forests and prevented forest fires and soil erosion. More than 100,000 Michiganians joined the CCC and worked all over the state. They made money to support their families, and they learned life skills that helped them get jobs in the years to come.

In 1939, World War II (1939–1945) erupted in Europe. The U.S. government came to the aid of its ally, Great Britain, by asking the Ford Motor Company to produce aircraft engines for the British war effort. Henry Ford refused the request. He believed that the United States should stay out of the war. In the meantime, William S. Knudsen, the head of General Motors (GM), became chairman of the National Defense Advisory Commission. And he worked with K. T. Keller of the Chrysler Corporation on a way to build tanks

WORD TO KNOW

sit-down strike *a refusal to work, while remaining at the place of employment*

for the war effort. Suddenly, Michigan was producing trucks, tanks, and other military supplies. The revived industry lifted Michigan out of the Great Depression at last. Finally, even Ford joined the effort when he built his Willow Run Bomber Plant near Ypsilanti.

After Japanese forces bombed the U.S. Navy base at Pearl Harbor on December 7, 1941, the United States entered the war. About 670,000 of Michigan's citizens joined the armed forces. At this time, most women were homemakers. As many men left their factory jobs to become soldiers, women had to fill in. Approximately 200,000 women worked in Michigan auto plants during these war years.

HEADING NORTH

Between 1910 and 1970, in what was called the Great Migration, about 6.5 million African Americans left the South and headed to northern cities for work. They knew that wages were higher in the North. And they heard that there was less **discrimination**. They could also vote more easily because there were no **poll taxes**.

By the 1940s, about 50,000 African Americans had moved to Detroit to work in factories producing military supplies. Life in the North may have been better than in the South, but people of color still faced discrimination. President Roosevelt had made it illegal for workers to be treated differently because of race or ethnicity. But for African Americans, finding good housing or quality education was nearly impossible. During this time, the Detroit chapter of the National Association for the Advancement of Colored People (NAACP) urged its members to stand up for their rights.

WORDS TO KNOW

discrimination *the act of treating people unfairly because of their race or other classification*

poll taxes *fees that people must pay before they can vote*

In June 1943, racial violence broke out on Belle Isle, in Detroit, and 34 people died. Over the next two decades, black Michiganians would again and again face racism and discrimination.

THE BOOM YEARS

After World War II, the state of Michigan enjoyed a healthy economy. At this time, just about every American wanted a car. Because the auto industry had almost no competition from other states or countries, Michigan's automakers became very wealthy. In 1955, the state's per capita income was 16 percent above the U.S. average—and among the highest in the world.

SEE IT HERE!

IDLEWILD

These days, Idlewild, Michigan, is a quiet town that has a museum and hosts music festivals. But from 1912 to the mid-1960s, it was one of the few U.S. resorts where African Americans could vacation and purchase land. Visitors swam, boated, hiked, and spent time with family and friends. As the resort grew more popular, top entertainers—such as Bill Cosby, Duke Ellington, Stevie Wonder, Della Reese, and Sammy Davis Jr.—performed there.

Police fired tear gas to disperse the crowd when racial violence broke out in Detroit in 1943.

The Mackinac Bridge is 26,372 feet (8,038 m) long and the roadway is about 200 feet (60 m) above the water at mid-span. It is the third-longest suspension bridge in the world.

Many miles of highways were constructed, and in 1957 the Mackinac Bridge was opened to traffic. This suspension bridge soared above the Straits of Mackinac and provided an easier way for people to travel between the Lower Peninsula and Upper Peninsula.

TRYING TIMES

During the 1940s and 1950s, more and more African Americans came to Detroit and other Michigan cities. They arrived hoping to find work and a place to call home. But they found themselves fighting for their **civil rights**. Many white citizens did not want them moving into their neighborhoods. Fights broke out in the streets and at the workplace.

On June 23, 1963, Martin Luther King Jr. visited Detroit for the Great March to Freedom. This event was the largest civil rights rally up to that time. About 125,000 people marched, carrying signs and singing "We Shall Overcome." At the end of the march, King gave his "I Have a Dream" speech. Two months later, he delivered a similar speech in Washington, D.C. It was one of the greatest moments in civil rights history.

WORDS TO KNOW

civil rights *the rights of personal liberty that are guaranteed to all citizens*

riot *public disorder or violence*

Picture Yourself . . .

Marching with Martin Luther King Jr.

It's the summer of 1963, and you are about to be part of history. The civil rights movement has been active in the South. And now Martin Luther King Jr. is in Detroit. You gather with thousands and thousands of other people, and you strain to find King in the crowd. You think you glimpse him, but you aren't quite sure. Then you and all the others march down Woodward Avenue. As you walk, you feel hot. But mostly you feel excited. And you're a little scared, too. What if a fight breaks out? But that doesn't happen.

The crowd ends the march at Cobo Hall, and there you hear King begin his speech. You hear him say, "I can assure you that what has been done here today will serve as a source of inspiration for all of the freedom-loving people of this nation." And you feel proud.

In July 1967, police arrested a group of African Americans in Detroit. A crowd gathered to protest social injustice and what they considered an unfair arrest. The protest turned into an outpouring of anger and frustration at their oppressive poverty when a **riot** broke out. People broke shop windows, and soon rioting spread throughout the neighborhood. By the second day, poor, discontented whites had joined in the looting. The riot lasted for five days. In what came to be called the 12th Street Riot, 43 people died and 7,200 were arrested. Violence spread to Grand Rapids, Pontiac, Flint, and

MINI-BIO

RALPH BUNCHE: WORLD DIPLOMAT

As a United Nations official, Detroit native Ralph Bunche (1904–1971) mediated between warring Palestinians and Israelis. His peace-seeking efforts won him the Nobel Peace Prize in 1950. Dr. Bunche was one of few Americans, and the first African American, to earn this honor. In 1965, he marched for equal voting rights with Martin Luther King Jr. in Selma, Alabama, an effort that led Congress to pass the Voting Rights Act that year. President Lyndon Johnson awarded Bunche the Medal of Freedom. Bunche once said, "I am proud of my ancestry just as I am proud of my nationality."

Want to know more? See http://nobelprize.org/nobel_prizes/peace/laureates/1950/bunche-bio.html

American civil rights leader Martin Luther King Jr. (front, third from right) leads a march against racial discrimination in Detroit in 1963.

other cities. In the decades to come, racial inequalities continued, but some progress was made.

Malcolm X was a human rights activist who grew up in the Lansing area. He encouraged African Americans to be proud of their heritage. Some of his opinions were considered controversial. He was assassinated in New York City in 1965.

As the nation endured **recessions** in the 1980s, the auto industry faced stiff competition from international carmakers. It is often cheaper to make cars in other countries than it is in the United States. So consumers often buy those less expensive cars. As a result of the increased competition from international carmakers, many Michigan autoworkers lost their jobs.

WORD TO KNOW

recessions *periods of reduced economic activity*

Burning storefronts during the 12th Street Riot of July 1967

In recent decades, many Michiganians have been in need of good jobs and opportunities to succeed.

After being so wealthy, Michigan now suffered more unemployment than any other state. Some towns, such as Flint, had an unemployment rate of more than 20 percent. The state per capita income—which was once so high—plummeted to almost 7 percent below the national average.

LOOKING FORWARD

It wasn't long before Michigan realized it had to rely on something other than auto manufacturing. It began concentrating on tourism and other industries. In 1977, Detroit added the Renaissance Center to its skyline. The Renaissance Center is a group of towers, and its central tower is the tallest building in Michigan. The complex houses a hotel, a conference center, and offices. The Renaissance Center helped revitalize Detroit, and its 2003 renovation made it more modern and up-to-date. The state also realized that there must be better ways to produce energy. In recent years, Michiganians have made great strides in experimenting with alternative fuels such as hydrogen and biodiesel. In the years to come, the state wants to rebuild its roads and upgrade other parts of its transportation system.

Life in Detroit and other Michigan cities has been challenging for some groups of people. Because of high crime rates and other problems, many people have left the cities to live in the suburbs. Towns have been affected, as well. Many small businesses that are tied to the automobile industry have seen their incomes

A crowd enjoys Jazz Fest, with the Renaissance Center as a backdrop.

In 2007, Michiganians celebrated the 50th anniversary of the opening of the Mackinac Bridge.

reduced. But Michiganians have never backed down from tough situations. People worked to make the cities safer and to encourage new businesses in the state. By 2000, the unemployment rate for Michigan was below 3 percent for the first time since records had been kept.

Michigan has much more to boast about, too. In 2001, Detroit celebrated its 300th anniversary with a parade of tall ships and a reenactment of the founding of the city. And in 2007, Michiganians celebrated the 50th anniversary of the mighty Mackinac Bridge. The work of the bridge maintenance crews was featured on the Discovery Channel's *Dirty Jobs* TV show. That same year, the Detroit Science Center opened an 80-foot (24 m) replica of the bridge. As the 21st century progresses, Michiganians continue to honor their past and look forward to their future.

READ ABOUT

Places to Learn 66

Music Capital 70

Michigan Writers 70

On Stage and Screen 72

Art and Artists 72

The Sports Arena 74

A crowd walks along the Detroit River during the city's International River Days.

PEOPLE

★

IF YOU VISITED MICHIGAN CITIES, TOWNS, AND SMALL VILLAGES, WHAT KINDS OF PEOPLE WOULD YOU SEE? All kinds. In Detroit and Dearborn, you might meet Arab families. In Holland, you might meet people whose ancestors came from the Netherlands. This state is made up of people whose families originally came from Europe, Central America, Africa, Asia, and many other places. Michigan is a colorful mosaic of artists and writers, executives and farmers, athletes and entrepreneurs, teachers and scientists. Its diversity helps make Michigan such an interesting place!

Big City Life

This list shows the population of Michigan's biggest cities.

Detroit	871,121
Grand Rapids	193,083
Warren	134,589
Sterling Heights	127,991
Flint	117,068
Lansing	114,276
Ann Arbor	113,206

Source: U.S. Census Bureau, 2006 estimates

LIFE IN THE CITY

Michigan's population ranks eighth in the nation. Most Michiganians live in and around cities in the southern Lower Peninsula. Detroit, Michigan's largest city, is one of the country's major industrial centers. In recent decades, the population of Detroit has actually decreased, as many people chose to move out of the city to nearby towns and suburbs.

Where Michiganians Live

The colors on this map indicate population density throughout the state. The darker the color, the more people live there.

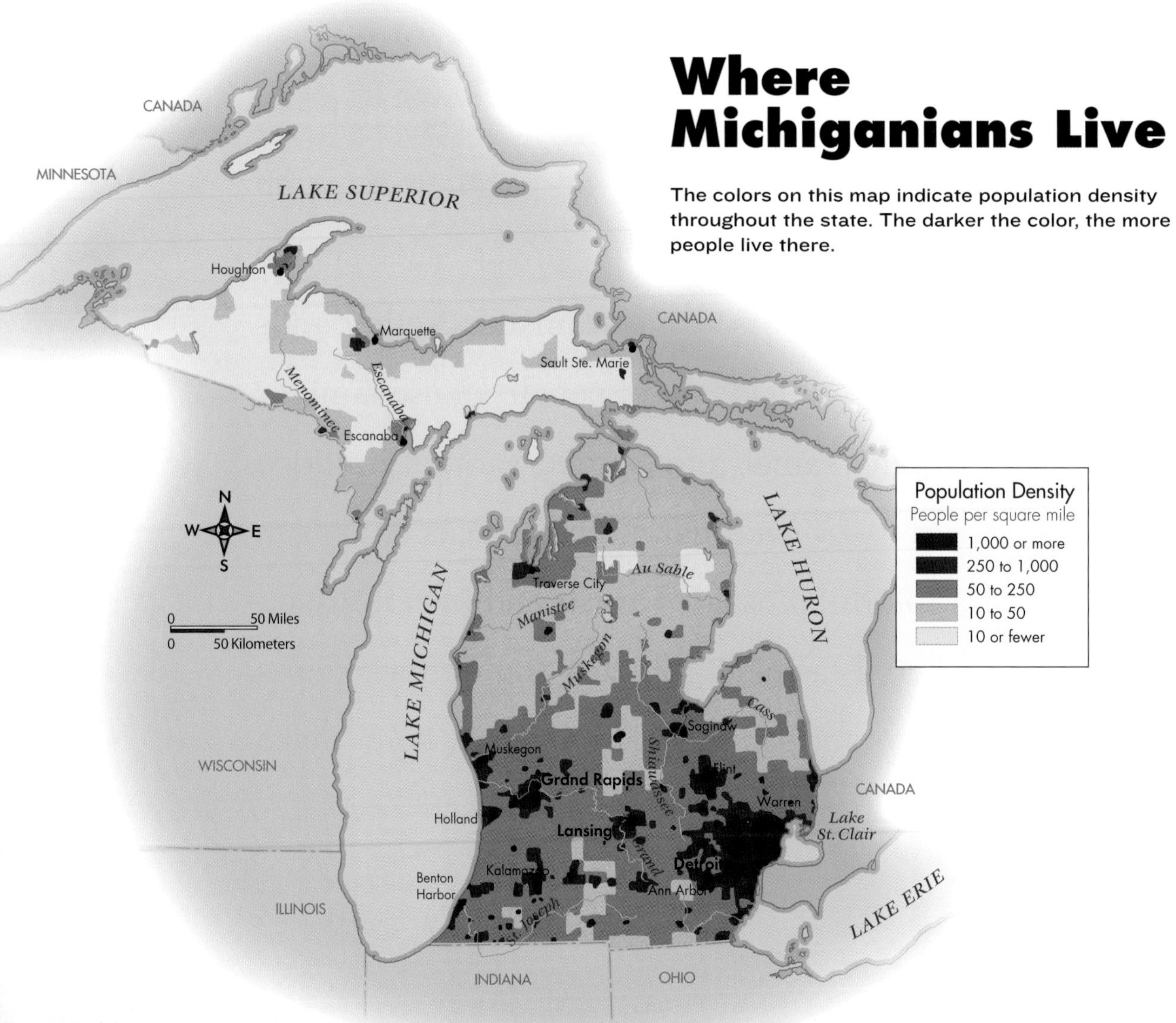

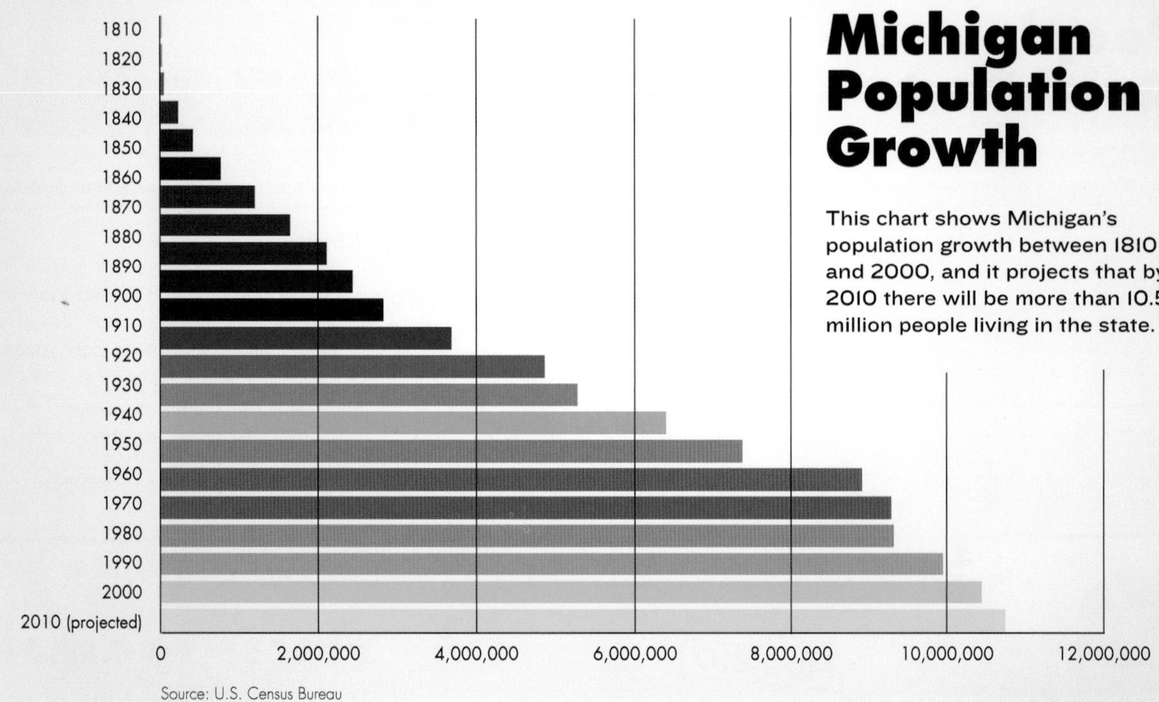

Michigan Population Growth

This chart shows Michigan's population growth between 1810 and 2000, and it projects that by 2010 there will be more than 10.5 million people living in the state.

Grand Rapids is the second-largest city, followed by Warren, which is a suburb of Detroit. In Flint, many businesses rely on automobile manufacturing, so this city has been hard-hit in the past several years.

Dearborn is home to the largest percentage of Arabs in any city outside the Middle East—30,000 out of 98,000 people. Dearborn is the headquarters of the Islamic Center of America, the largest mosque in the United States, and the Arab American National Museum. In fact, Dearborn has many signs in English and Arabic.

An Arabic sign in Dearborn

People QuickFacts

White, not Hispanic: 77.9%
Black persons: 14.3%*
Persons of Hispanic or Latino origin: 3.8%†
Asian persons: 2.2%*
American Indian and Alaska Native persons: 0.6%*
Persons reporting two or more races: 1.5%

*Includes persons reporting only one race.
†Hispanics may be of any race, so they are also included in applicable race categories.
Source: U.S. Census Bureau, 2006 estimate

MINI-BIO

FANNIE RICHARDS: TEACHER AND ACTIVIST

Some say she was ahead of her time. Fannie Richards (c. 1840–1922) was the first African American public school teacher in Detroit. She was born in Virginia, but in 1863 she opened a school for African American children in Detroit. She then went on to teach in the public school system. In 1869, she helped bring a lawsuit against the city's segregated school system. As a result, the Michigan Supreme Court ordered Detroit schools to integrate. In 1871, Richards began working at the Everett Elementary School and taught the city's first kindergarten class. She retired in 1915 after more than 50 years as a teacher.

Want to know more? See www.michiganhistorymagazine.com/extra/women/richards.html

PLACES TO LEARN

In 1835, Michigan became the first state to create a public education system headed by a superintendent, which is how most school systems in the country are run today. And in 1874, it was the first state to determine that high schools were part of the school system. Today, public schools are supported by local school districts and by state funds. Children who are ages 6 to 16 are required to attend. About 10 percent of Michigan kids attend private schools.

As of 2007, Michigan had 43 public and 51 private institutions of higher learning.

Students on the University of Michigan campus

Michigan State University was founded after the state constitution of 1850 called for the formation of an agricultural school. The University of Michigan has one of the largest libraries in the nation. And the Gerald R. Ford Presidential Library is located on campus. Other colleges and universities include Wayne State University in Detroit; Hope College in Holland; Kalamazoo College and Western Michigan University in Kalamazoo; Northern Michigan University in Marquette; Central Michigan University in Mount Pleasant Eastern Michigan University in Ypsilanti; and Oakland University in Rochester.

MINI-BIO

HELEN THOMAS: FIRST LADY OF THE PRESS

As a journalist, Helen Thomas (1920–) covered John F. Kennedy in the White House—and eight presidents since. She attended Detroit public schools and graduated from Wayne State University in 1942. In 1972, she was the only female print journalist to travel to China with President Nixon. Over the years, Thomas has gained a reputation for asking the "tough questions," and some presidents have tried to avoid talking to her! In 1998, she was the first recipient of the Helen Thomas Lifetime Achievement Award, an honor that White House correspondents established in her name.

Want to know more? See www.michiganhistorymagazine.com/extra/women/

HOW TO TALK LIKE A MICHIGANIAN

What's a yooper? Well, that's a Michigan term for someone who lives in the Upper Peninsula (the UP). And what's a troll? A person who lives in the Lower Peninsula, since yoopers think people from the Lower Peninsula live "under the bridge."

In the southern United States, if you're talking to a group of friends, you might call them "y'all." But in Michigan, you're more likely to refer to the group as "you guys."

And if you want to order a soft drink, what do you do? You ask for a "pop."

HOW TO EAT LIKE A MICHIGANIAN

Eating in Michigan can be a real treat. There are fresh apples, cherries, and other produce to enjoy. And you'll find great German and Polish food in many neighborhoods. If you like fish, you can enjoy the day's catch from the Great Lakes. Vernor's ginger ale has a unique tart taste. It was invented in 1866 in Detroit, sharing the title (with Hires root beer) as the country's oldest soft drink.

Amish women arrange fresh strawberries at a farmers market near Lexington

MENU

WHAT'S ON THE MENU IN MICHIGAN?

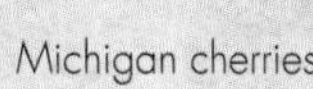

Michigan cherries

Lake Fish

The Great Lakes State is bound to have lots of lake fish—particularly whitefish and lake perch. You can get it broiled, fried, smoked, or on top of a salad.

The Pasty

A traditional food of the Upper Peninsula. It's made with meat, onions, potatoes, and optional rutabaga, all wrapped up in a light dough. And be sure to pronounce it like "nasty," not "hasty."

Senate Bean Soup

This recipe from Michigan is on the menu at the U.S. Senate dining room every day. It's made with dried Michigan navy beans, ham hocks, and onions.

Apple Cider

It's made from Michigan's bountiful apple harvest. Great hot or cold!

Apple cider

TRY THIS RECIPE

Cherry Corn Muffins

What says "Michigan" more than beautiful red cherries? The state produces more than 70 percent of the tart cherries grown in the United States and 20 percent of the sweet variety. So try out this recipe and savor one of Michigan's local flavors. But be sure to have an adult nearby to help.

Ingredients:

¾ cup yellow cornmeal
1 ¼ cups all-purpose flour
⅔ cup dried tart cherries
½ cup granulated sugar
2 teaspoons baking powder
¼ teaspoon salt
1 cup milk
¼ cup vegetable oil
1 egg, slightly beaten
1 teaspoon vanilla extract

Instructions:

1. Preheat the oven to 400°F.
2. Place 12 paper muffin cups in muffin tins.
3. Combine cornmeal, flour, cherries, sugar, baking powder, and salt in a mixing bowl, and mix well.
4. Stir in milk, oil, egg, and vanilla until the mixture is moist.
5. Fill each muffin cup about three-quarters full with batter.
6. Bake 20–25 minutes. Test by poking muffins with a toothpick. If it comes out clean, the muffins are ready.
7. Let cool in pan 5 minutes before serving.

Cherry corn muffins

MUSIC CAPITAL

In the 1950s, an automobile worker named Berry Gordy left his job on the Ford Lincoln Mercury assembly line so he could pursue a career in music. In 1959, this Detroit songwriter founded Motown Records. Smokey Robinson and the Miracles was one of the first acts he signed. Together with Robinson, Aretha Franklin, Marvin Gaye, Diana Ross and the Supremes, Stevie Wonder, and other great musicians, Gordy created the Motown sound.

In 2004, the Rock and Roll Hall of Fame inducted Detroit's Bob Seger, whose songs reflect the blue-collar lives of so many Michiganians. Fellow Detroiter Kid Rock gave the presentation speech. Rapper Eminem often writes lyrics that capture the difficulty of growing up on the gritty side of the city.

MINI-BIO

STEVIE WONDER: MUSIC MAN

Born in Saginaw, Stevie Wonder (1950–) moved to Detroit at a young age. When he was just 11 years old, he signed a contract with Berry Gordy at Motown Records. He had his first hit at age 13. He was born blind, but it's never kept him from following his dreams.

Some of his fans' favorite songs are "You Are the Sunshine of My Life" and "I Just Called to Say I Love You," which won an Academy Award. It also became Motown's best-selling single!

Over the years, Wonder has won dozens of Grammy Awards. Wonder's songs celebrate peace and love, and he has voiced concern over the violent aspects of some contemporary music. Many musicians—such as Mariah Carey, Alicia Keys, Maroon 5, Prince, and Beyoncé—describe him as a major influence in their careers.

Want to know more? See www.steviewonder.net

MICHIGAN WRITERS

Chris Van Allsburg was born and raised in Grand Rapids. The street on the cover of his Caldecott-winning *The Polar Express* (1985) looks like one of the streets he grew up on. Patricia Polacco, author of *Thank You, Mr. Faulkner* (1998) and *Chicken Sunday* (1992), was born in Lansing and now lives in Union City in a house that was once a station on the Underground Railroad. Author Christopher Paul Curtis was born in Flint and worked on an assembly line hanging car doors for 13 years. He has written the novels *The Watsons Go to Birmingham—1963* (1997)

Christopher Paul Curtis was an autoworker before he became an award-winning children's author.

and *Bud, Not Buddy* (1999), which was the first book ever to win both a Newbery Medal and a Coretta Scott King Author Award. Another writer for young readers, Gloria Whalen, was born in Detroit and now lives in northern Michigan. She often writes about her home state. She won a National Book Award for *Homeless Bird* (2000), about a young girl in India.

Classic Michigan authors include Ring Lardner (1885–1933), a sportswriter with a witty style; Edna Ferber (1885–1968), who wrote novels and short stories; and Theodore Roethke (1908–1963), who wrote masterful poems about his Saginaw childhood and won the Pulitzer Prize in 1954.

Another best-selling writer who lives in Michigan is Mitch Albom, a sportswriter for the *Detroit Free Press*. He has also written *Tuesdays with Morrie* (1997), among other best sellers. Thomas Lynch of Milford is not only a poet and a commentator for National Public Radio, but he is also the local funeral director. One of his books, *The Undertaking* (1997), was nominated for a National Book Award.

MINI-BIO

DANNY THOMAS: ACTOR AND HUMANITARIAN

He starred on TV's *Make Room for Daddy*, but today Danny Thomas (1912–1991) is also remembered for founding the St. Jude Children's Research Hospital in Memphis, Tennessee. He was born Amos Alphonsus Muzyad Yakhoob in Deerfield, Michigan. In 1962, he founded St. Jude, a world-class hospital and research center that treats children with cancer and other diseases.

Want to know more? See www.stjude.org

ON STAGE AND SCREEN

The Grand Rapids Civic Theater is the second-largest community theater in the United States. It produces a variety of plays and children's shows each year. In Lansing, you can enjoy plays at the BoarsHead Theater, the Riverwalk Theatre, and the Spotlight Theatre in nearby Grand Ledge.

Detroit native Tim Allen is known to TV watchers and moviegoers all over the world. He was the voice of Buzz Lightyear in *Toy Story* (1995) and *Toy Story 2* (1999). He also starred in *Home Improvement* on TV and in the *Santa Clause* movies.

Michael Moore is a controversial **documentary** filmmaker who was born in Flint. His movie *Roger and Me* (1989) took a look at General Motors and the effect the company had on Moore's hometown. Other films include *Fahrenheit 9/11* (2004), *Bowling for Columbine* (2002), which earned him an Academy Award, and *Sicko* (2007).

WORD TO KNOW

documentary *something that is factual and shows real lifee*

ART AND ARTISTS

In 1932, Edsel Ford, then president of the Ford Motor Company, commissioned Mexican painter Diego Rivera to create two murals for the Detroit Institute of Art. *Detroit Industry* is a masterpiece that features workers of all races in various industries.

Lewis Thomas Ives was a portrait artist from Rochester, New York, who lived and worked in Detroit. Loja Saarinen was a textile worker and sculptor. She was born in Finland but came to Cranbrook Academy of Art, a renowned art museum and school in Bloomfield Hills, in 1924. Her husband, Eliel, was an architect who designed the Cranbrook campus and served as its president.

MINI-BIO

MARSHALL FREDERICKS: SPIRITED SCULPTOR

Although he was born in Illinois, sculptor Marshall Fredericks (1908–1998) was one of Detroit's favorite artists. He began teaching at Cranbrook Academy of Art in 1932, and Michigan quickly became his home. In 1936, he won a competition to create a sculpture for Detroit's Belle Isle. The majestic *Leaping Gazelle* became the first of his many public monuments. *Spirit of Detroit* graces the Coleman A. Young Municipal Center in Detroit. It is 26 feet (8 m) tall and is a local landmark. It even "wears" jerseys of local teams when they make the playoffs.

Much of his work appears outside of Michigan, as well. He created *Freedom of the Human Spirit* for the 1963 World's Fair in New York City and *The Expanding Universe Fountain* for the State Department building in Washington, D.C. Today, the Marshall M. Fredericks Sculpture Museum is a part of Saginaw Valley State University.

Want to know more? See www.svsu.edu/mfsm/

SEE IT HERE!

INTERLOCHEN CENTER FOR THE ARTS

Want to visit a gallery or see a great play? Or how about an outdoor concert? Michigan is the place. The state is home to the Interlochen Center for the Arts near Traverse City. This incredible facility has a summer camp and year-round programs in writing, music, dance, theater, and visual arts. Its festivals offer a wide assortment of plays and concerts that are open to the public.

THE SPORTS ARENA

Michigan is home to a number of great athletes and outstanding teams. The Detroit Lions have been wowing football fans for decades. Barry Sanders was a star running back for the Lions and played for them his entire career—from 1989 to 1999.

The Detroit Pistons won the National Basketball Association championship in 1989, 1990, and 2004. All-star guard Joe Dumars played for the Pistons from 1985 to 1999, and in 2000, he became president of basketball operations for the team.

The Detroit Tigers have played a big part in baseball history. They were founded in 1894 as a charter member of the American League. The Tigers have won the World Series four times. Baseball Hall of Famer Ty Cobb played for the Tigers from 1905 to 1926, and he was the team manager for six years.

On the ice, the Detroit Red Wings have won the Stanley Cup ten times! Hockey great Gordie Howe was born in Canada, but he was an all-star player for the Redwings from 1946 to 1971.

Detroit is also home to the Arsenal, a soccer team in the National Premier Soccer League; the Shock, with the Women's National Basketball Association; and the Fury, part of the Arena Football League.

MINI-BIO

SHELLEY LOONEY: ICE QUEEN

She shoots—she scores! Shelley Looney (1972–) was born in Brownstown Township and played hockey at Northeastern University. Then she was part of the U.S. team at the 1998 Winter Olympic Games in Nagano, Japan. In six Olympic matches, she scored a total of five goals—and one was the game winner against Canada. That earned the Americans a gold medal! In 2002, she was a member of the U.S. Olympic team that brought home the silver medal. The following year, Looney joined the National Team Development Program in Ann Arbor. What a great way for her to pass her knowledge on to young hockey players.

Want to know more? See www.gonu.com/hall/looney.html

Michigan colleges have lots of sports fans, too. The University of Michigan and Michigan State University boast football and basketball powerhouses.

Sports greats from Michigan include Derek Jeter and Joe Louis. Jeter was born in New Jersey, but graduated from Kalamazoo Central High School and attended the University of Michigan. These days, he's the all-star shortstop for the New York Yankees. Louis was born in Alabama but raised in Detroit. He became the boxing heavyweight champion of the world in 1937 and held the title for 12 years. On the playing field or on stage, at work and at school, Michiganians have made their mark in the world.

The Michigan State University Spartans women's basketball team celebrates a victory over the Tennessee Lady Vols in 2005.

READ ABOUT

How the Government Works 78

The Executive Branch 81

The Legislative Branch 82

The Judicial Branch 83

The Voice of the People 85

The Michigan state capitol is a national historic landmark. It is the third building to house the state government.

GOVERNMENT

★

THE NORTHWEST ORDINANCE OF 1787 REQUIRED THAT EACH TERRITORY HAVE A CONSTITUTION TO BECOME A STATE. So, in 1835, delegates met in Detroit to draft a constitution. The delegates created a bill of rights (but only white men at least 21 years of age could vote) and split the government into three branches: executive, legislative, and judicial. Michigan citizens would elect a governor, lieutenant governor, and legislators. The governor would appoint key department heads and supreme court judges, with help from the senate.

HOW THE GOVERNMENT WORKS

By 1850, Michiganians' feelings about appointed officials had changed, so they wrote a revised constitution. Under this constitution, the secretary of state, attorney general, auditor general, and supreme court justices were elected rather than appointed. Today, the state is governed by the constitution of 1963, which has been amended 25 times.

How do people learn how government works? In Michigan, middle school and high school students can participate in Youth in Government. This program is sponsored by the state YMCA. Its participants meet at the capitol in Lansing and take part in legislative sessions. Each student has to write and present a bill about an issue in the state. As former governor John Engler explains, "Youth in Government is truly an extraordinary educational opportunity. There is no better way for you to learn about the workings of democracy than by actively participating in it."

WOW

Michigan has an official children's book! *The Legend of Sleeping Bear*, by Kathy-Jo Wargin, is a retelling of an Ojibwa tale. The book was recognized by the Michigan house of representatives in 1998.

The state capitol in Lansing

CENTER OF GOVERNMENT

When Michigan became a state in 1835, its capital was Detroit. But in 1847, that changed when the capital moved to Lansing. Back then, some people preferred Detroit because it was more modern and easier to get to. But other people thought the capital should be closer to the center of the state. So after much debate, Lansing was chosen, and the once-rugged frontier land was transformed into a capital city.

Capitol Facts

Here are some fascinating facts about Michigan's state capitol.

The Michigan capitol was designed by architect Elijah E. Myers. Construction began in 1873, and the building was dedicated on January 1, 1879.

Height . . . . .267 feet (81.4 m)
Length . . . . .420 feet 2 inches (128 m)
Width . . . . 273 feet 11 inches (83.5 m)
Dome. . . . . Made of cast iron and features paintings of the muses (goddesses of artistic inspiration) dating to 1886

The capitol was named a national historic landmark on October 7, 1992.

Capital City

This map shows places of interest in Lansing, Michigan's capital city.

Michigan State Government

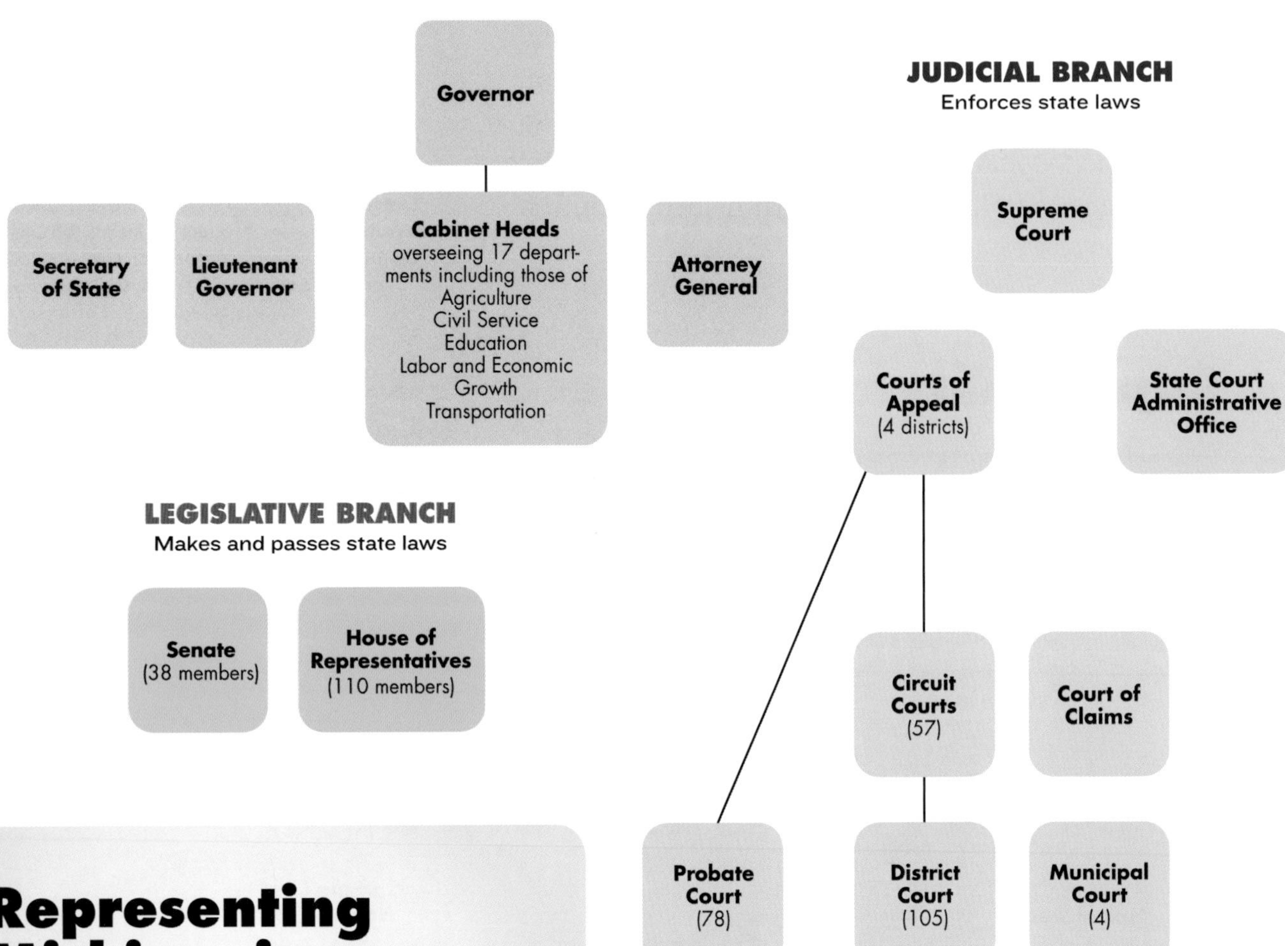

Representing Michiganians

This list shows the number of elected officials who represent Michigan, both on the state and national levels.

OFFICE	NUMBER	LENGTH OF TERM
State senators	38	4 years
State representatives	110	2 years
U.S. senators	2	6 years
U.S. representatives	15	2 years
Presidential electors	17	—

THE EXECUTIVE BRANCH

According to the constitution of 1963, the executive branch is made up of a governor, a lieutenant governor, and various departments. The governor and lieutenant governor are elected every four years and can serve just two terms. Their main job is to enforce laws and maintain order. The governor also submits a budget to the Michigan legislature. He or she appoints people to certain government committees.

Some appointees include the state treasurer, the superintendent of public instruction, and the head of the highway commission. In the mid-1990s, there were some changes made to the departments of the executive branch. For instance, a Department of Environmental Quality was created.

In case of emergency—such as a riot or a natural disaster—the governor can call up the state's military for help. In addition, the governor serves as a promoter of the state, encouraging tourism and new businesses for Michigan.

MINI-BIO

MADAM GOVERNOR: JENNIFER M. GRANHOLM

When she was elected to the office in 2002, Jennifer Granholm (1959–) became Michigan's first female governor. She was born in Vancouver, British Columbia, in Canada. In 1986, she married Daniel Mulhern and moved to his native state of Michigan. She began serving the Eastern District of Michigan as an assistant U.S. attorney in 1990. Eight years later, she was elected attorney general for Michigan. She was the first woman to hold this job.

After becoming governor, Granholm faced a lot of challenges in Michigan. Many people were unemployed, and the economy in the state was suffering. But Governor Granholm is trying to help her state improve. She was reelected as governor in 2006.

Want to know more? See www.michigan.gov/gov

THE LEGISLATIVE BRANCH

This part of the Michigan government is made up of a 38-member senate and a 110-member house of representatives. Senators are elected to four-year terms. Representatives are elected to two-year terms. The legislature has a number of committees that specialize in certain types of issues, from farming to education. When both parts of the legislature approve a bill, it goes to the governor for his or her signature before becoming state law. The governor can sign the bill or **veto** it. But the legislature can then override that veto if it has enough votes.

WORD TO KNOW

veto *to reject a proposed law*

MINI-BIO

JOHN CONYERS JR.: LONG-STANDING LEADER

Detroit native John Conyers Jr. (1929–) was elected to the House of Representatives in 1964 and has been there ever since! He was a founding member of the Congressional Black Caucus, and he is chairman of the House Judiciary Committee. Conyers went to Detroit public schools and graduated from Wayne State University in Detroit. Throughout his career, he has been a strong voice for civil rights. He has also focused on issues that concern women.

Want to know more? See www.house.gov/conyers/

FAQ

Q: WHO WAS MICHIGAN'S FIRST WOMAN IN CONGRESS?

A: Her name was Ruth Thompson (1887–1970), and she was born in Whitehall. Thompson was a Muskegon County judge who served in the U.S. House of Representatives from 1951 to 1957.

A circuit judge appears before the Michigan supreme court during a public hearing.

WACKY LAWS

It's hard to believe that some of these laws could ever have been written! But they are still on the books in Michigan. Let's just hope they are no longer enforced.

- It is illegal for a woman to cut her hair without getting her husband's permission.
- It is illegal for a man to kiss his wife on Sunday.
- In Detroit, it is against the law to let your pig run free in the street—unless it has a ring in its nose.
- And throughout the state, it is illegal to chain your alligator to a fire hydrant.

THE JUDICIAL BRANCH

Courts and juries are both part of the judicial branch of the government. Judges run the courts and make sure juries learn all they need to about a given legal case. These judges are part of the 57 **circuit courts** in Michigan.

Michigan's state supreme court has seven judges. These men and women are elected to eight-year terms, and they choose one of their members to be chief justice. The supreme court is the highest court in Michigan.

Other types of courts in Michigan are the courts of appeal, probate courts, district courts, and municipal courts. The courts of appeal hear cases that have already been decided and are being reconsidered. The probate courts protect the rights of people who died and make sure their instructions are carried out. And the district courts and municipal courts deal with less serious problems, such as parking tickets.

WORD TO KNOW

circuit courts *courts that are located at two or more places in one judicial district*

FREEDOM FIGHTERS

Michigan courts try important cases every day. But in 1925, there was a court case that made history. Frank Murphy was an Irish American judge in Detroit. Dr. Ossian Sweet was an African American scientist who had studied radium and radioactivity with Marie Curie, a famous scientist who had won a Nobel Prize in 1903. When Murphy and Sweet met in a Detroit courtroom in 1925, they changed the fight for justice in Michigan and the United States. Sweet was charged with murder, and Murphy was the judge.

Sweet had bought a home in a white Detroit neighborhood. He heard that his new neighbors were furious, so he gave them time to calm down. After nine months, he moved his family in, but his white neighbors had not adjusted. As angry mobs gathered outside,

A Michigan historic marker, outside the Ossian Sweet House, tells the story of the famous trial.

Sweet, fearing for the safety of his family, brought in friends and some guns. When the mob attacked with guns and stones, Sweet returned fire. When a bullet killed a white man, police burst into the house and arrested Sweet and his wife for murder.

Sweet's lawyer, Clarence Darrow, easily proved that the mob had threatened Sweet's home and his family. Judge Murphy reminded the jury that a person—of any color—has a right to defend his home. Sweet was declared innocent, and all charges were dropped. The Sweets returned home to live in peace with their white neighbors.

Frank Murphy was elected mayor of Detroit and then governor of Michigan. In 1937, Murphy, a champion of labor union rights, settled a major auto strike peacefully. President Franklin D. Roosevelt appointed Murphy to the U.S. Supreme Court. When Japanese American families were thrust into internment camps during World War II, Murphy warned that the United States was sinking into "the ugly abyss of racism." He was called the "most consistent [Supreme Court] voice for kindness, tolerance and humanity."

THE VOICE OF THE PEOPLE

Throughout Michigan's 83 counties, there are local governments. Small villages and big cities all have courts and councils that allow the voice of the people to be heard.

Michigan voters adopted two important changes in the 1990s. In 1992, they added term limits to the state constitution. These restrict state representatives to three terms in office, which means no more than six years. Other major elected officials—state senators, the governor, the lieutenant governor, the secretary of state, and the attorney general—are limited to two terms, or a total of eight years. In 1994, voters approved big changes in school funding. They voted to make school funding more equal throughout the state by raising the statewide sales tax and at the same time lowering the local property taxes that had supported the schools.

MINI-BIO

GERALD FORD: MICHIGAN PRESIDENT

Gerald Ford (1913–2006) grew up in Grand Rapids and was a star football player at the University of Michigan. During World War II, he served on an aircraft carrier. In 1948, he was elected as a Republican to the U.S. House of Representatives. He was reelected 12 times!

He was serving in Congress when Vice President Spiro Agnew had to resign in 1973. President Richard Nixon asked Ford to be vice president. Then, just a year later, Nixon left the presidency because of his role in the Watergate scandal. So Gerald Ford was suddenly the 38th president of the United States. He is the only U.S. president who was not elected either president or vice president.

In 1976, Ford ran against Jimmy Carter for the presidency and lost. This ended his political career. He died on December 26, 2006.

Want to know more? See www.whitehouse.gov/history/presidents/gf38.html

This Michigan citizen is voting in a local and national election at an elementary school in Battle Creek.

No matter what political party is in charge or who serves as governor, Michiganians know that they have a place in their government. They are not afraid to voice their opinions or change things that don't work.

Coleman Young was the mayor of Detroit for 20 years (1974–1994)! He was the first African American to hold the job.

Michigan Counties

This map shows the 83 counties in Michigan. Lansing, the state capital, is indicated with a star.

State Flag

The Michigan flag features the Great Seal set against a blue background. The state legislature adopted the flag in 1911.

State Seal

The Great Seal of Michigan shows some of Michigan's native animals. There is an elk on the left and a moose on the right, both supporting a shield that reads *Tuebor*. That means, "I will defend" in Latin. Inside the shield is the sun rising over a lake and a man standing on a peninsula. He has his right hand raised, symbolizing peace. But he holds a rifle in his left hand, which shows that he also stands ready to defend the state and nation.

Below the shield is the state motto, *Si quaeris peninsulam amoenam circumspice*. That's Latin for, "If you seek a pleasant peninsula, look about you." Above the shield is an American eagle and the motto of the United States, *E pluribus unum*, meaning "Out of many, one."

Lewis Cass, the second governor of the Michigan Territory, designed the seal, and the 1835 constitutional convention approved it.

READ ABOUT

Early Economy. 92

Building the Car. 94

Other Industry. 98

Bounty from Michigan Farmlands. . . . 99

Michigan in the Air. 100

Looking Forward. . . . 103

A Ford assembly line putting together the 2005 models of the Ford Mustang

CHAPTER EIGHT

ECONOMY

★

WHEN MOST PEOPLE THINK OF MICHIGAN, THEY THINK OF CARS. In fact, Michigan leads the nation in automobile production. And the state is home to the Big Three: General Motors, Ford Motor Company, and Chrysler. But Michigan also produces other things, such as breakfast cereal, paper, pharmaceuticals, and lumber. And Michigan farmers supply beans, corn, soybeans, cherries, and lots of other foods to the rest of the country. You might be surprised to find out that you use some Michigan products every day!

EARLY ECONOMY

When Europeans first came to Michigan, they made a living by fur trapping and trading. As the region became more populated in the first half of the 19th century, settlers began selling lumber and farming.

Michigan's climate and fertile soil helped it become a national leader in wheat production. Other crops became plentiful, as well. Fruit grew along the **temperate** Lake Michigan shoreline, and celery flourished in the Kalamazoo area.

After the Civil War, lumber became a huge industry. Michigan woodlands produced about a quarter of the nation's total supply. That production helped encourage furniture manufacturing in Grand Rapids and papermaking in Kalamazoo.

What did you have for breakfast this morning? If it was cereal, you may want to thank Will Keith (W. K.) Kellogg or Charles William (C. W.) Post. Kellogg first began producing flaked cereal when he was working with his brother, John Harvey Kellogg, at a hospital in Battle Creek. They showed their process to C. W. Post, who went on to create his own cereal. His company, Post Cereal, later became General Foods. Meanwhile, the Kelloggs worked to encourage people to eat healthy cereal for breakfast. In 1906, W. K. added sugar to the recipe for their cereal. John Harvey strongly disapproved.

As railroads were built, Michigan's economy strengthened. Railroads made it easier to deliver the state's lumber, cereal, and other products. Soon, mining operations began throughout the state. The metals mined in Michigan helped make the state a center for producing automobiles and their parts.

WORD TO KNOW

temperate *marked by moderation; mild*

Kellogg was one of the first food producers to include nutritional information on its boxes.

Major Agricultural and Mining Products

This map shows where Michigan's major agricultural and mining products come from. See an apple and pear? That means fruit is grown there.

TOP PRODUCTS

Agriculture
Dairy products, greenhouse and nursery plants, soybeans, cucumbers, cherries, apples, celery

Manufacturing
Automobiles, furniture, paper, cereal

Mining
Iron ore, limestone, natural gas, salt

Fishing
Whitefish, trout, salmon, yellow perch, carp

Henry Ford with his Model T automobile

In 1908, a Model T cost $825. By the 1920s, its cost had fallen to about $300 (that's around $3,300 today).

BUILDING THE CAR

In the late 1800s, most people got around by horse or on foot. But that was about to change. In fact, the invention of the automobile probably affected the lives of U.S. citizens more than any other development. In 1896, Charles King drove a four-cylinder "horseless carriage" down Woodward Avenue in Detroit. Later that year, Henry Ford and Ransom Olds drove their own models. Before long, the Olds became the first car to be produced in significant numbers. That success spurred other manufacturers to produce cars, as well.

In 1908, Henry Ford introduced the Model T. This car had a 15-horsepower engine and could go as fast as 45 miles per hour (72 kph). It was available only in black. Ford also developed assembly lines that proved key in mass production. Other people knew how to build cars, but Ford found a way to make them faster. More than 15 million Model Ts were built, and they transformed American transportation.

In 1908, William C. Durant of Flint founded the General Motors Corporation (GM). By the 1920s, it was the world leader in the production of automobiles. Other notable names in the auto industry were John F. and Horace E. Dodge. For a time, they built car parts to supply the Olds Motor Company. And they later supplied parts to the Ford Motor Company. In 1914, they began producing their own models of cars and trucks.

Over the years, the automobile industry has been closely tied to the general economic outlook in the United States. So, for instance, when lots of people are unemployed, the car industry suffers. In the 1970s, this industry went

MINI-BIO

ELIJAH MCCOY: INVENTOR

A son of runaway slaves, Michigan inventor Elijah McCoy (1843–1929) held 57 patents on significant inventions. His lubricator cup was "the real McCoy"—a phrase that now refers to anything that is genuine. Many of his devices were designed to save lives by automatically **lubricating** locomotives, engines, steamships, and factory machinery. Previously, this was done by hand. Many people doing the work lost limbs—or even their lives. In 1975, Detroit celebrated Elijah McCoy Day, and a street has been named for him.

Want to know more? See www.blackinventor.com/pages/elijahmccoy.html

WORD TO KNOW

lubricating *making smooth or slippery as a way to reduce friction and heat*

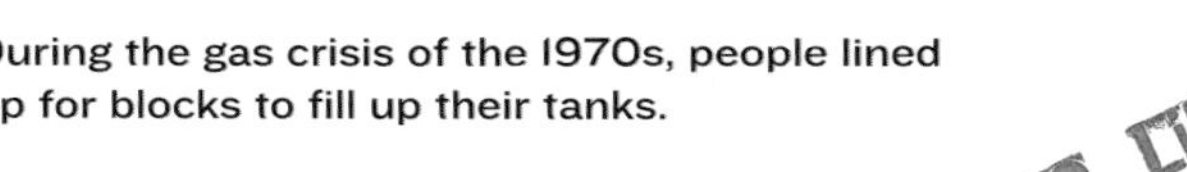

During the gas crisis of the 1970s, people lined up for blocks to fill up their tanks.

through a major crisis. As fuel prices rose, many customers decided against big American cars. They bought fuel-efficient imported models instead.

In the years since, the Big Three carmakers have had ups and downs. Increased competition from foreign carmakers is a challenging issue. Also, every company in the automotive industry is working to develop cars that are more fuel efficient and that run on alternative fuel sources, such as biodeisel.

Think About It: Restricting Foreign Imports

PRO

Some people believe that the United States should protect American carmakers from foreign trade. Rick Wagoner, chairman and CEO of General Motors Corporation, explains, "Some say we're looking for a bailout. Baloney—we at GM do not want a bailout. What we want—after we take the actions we are taking, in product, technology, cost and every area we're working in our business today—is the chance to compete on a level playing field. It's critical that government leaders, supported by business, unions and all our citizens, forge policy solutions to the issues undercutting American manufacturing competitiveness."

CON

Other people believe that American car manufacturers need to work harder to produce the kind of cars that American consumers want to buy. Daniel T. Griswold, director of the Center for Trade Policy Studies at Washington's Cato Institute, says, "There are plenty of reasons behind the troubles at GM, but 'unfair' competition from Japanese automakers is not among them. Japanese brands have certainly been gaining market share in the United States, but that has arguably more to do with the more appealing design, price, and quality of the cars than exchange rates."

Sources: *The Wall Street Journal*, November 6, 2005; Knight Ridder, June 26, 2005

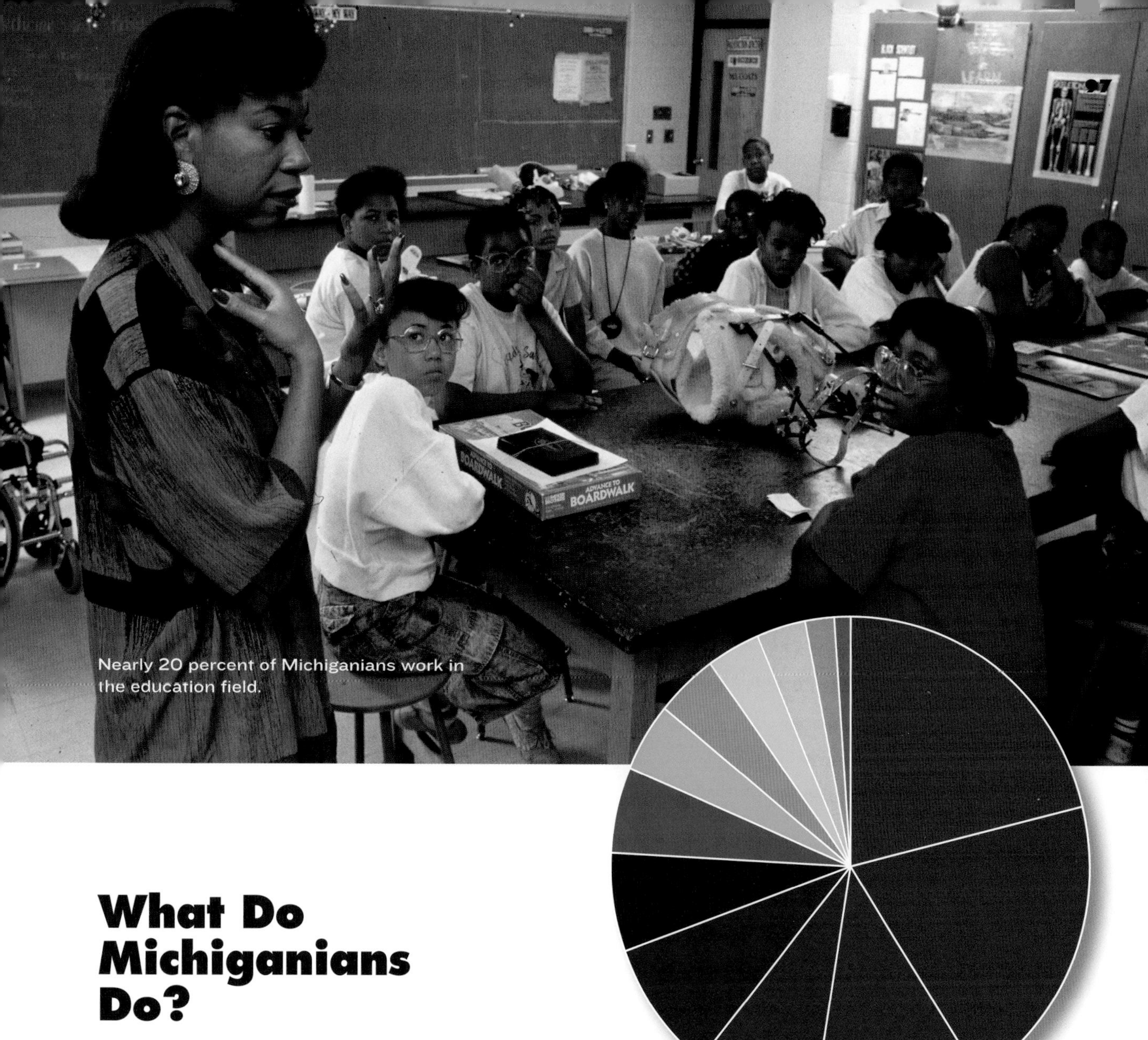

Nearly 20 percent of Michiganians work in the education field.

What Do Michiganians Do?

This color-coded chart shows what industries Michiganians work in.

Percent	Industry
21.2%	Educational services, and health care, and social assistance, 963,664
19.7%	Manufacturing, 895,443
11.7%	Retail trade, 529,641
8.5%	Arts, entertainment, and recreation, and accommodation and food services, 384,405
8.4%	Professional, scientific, and management, and administrative and waste management services, 382,603
6.4%	Construction, 292,662
5.6%	Finance and insurance, and real estate and rental and leasing, 254,356
4.5%	Other services, except public administration, 205,139
4.2%	Transportation and warehousing, and utilities, 188,159
3.6%	Public administration, 161,447
3.3%	Wholesale trade, 147,338
1.9%	Information, 87,038
1.0%	Agriculture, forestry, fishing and hunting, and mining, 47,120

Source: U.S. Census Bureau

MINI-BIO

HAREN GANDHI: TECHNO-GENIUS

As a Ford Technical Fellow at the Ford Motor Company in Dearborn, Haren Gandhi (1941–) has dedicated his career to making cars run more cleanly. He joined Ford in 1967 as a researcher. Since then, he has published more than 70 papers on technology and has been credited with more than 40 new patents. Gandhi won the 2002 National Medal of Technology, becoming the first person from the automotive industry to earn the award. He was recognized for helping develop and improve the automotive **exhaust system**. His work cuts down on **emissions**, making the air we all breathe cleaner.

Want to know more? See www.viaindia.com/articles/inspirational/haren.htm

INDUSTRY

Of course, there is more to Michigan's industry than cars. The state produces computers, missiles, and communications equipment. And these days, much of Michigan's economy relies on service industries such as printers, publishers, hotels, hospitals, restaurants, and real estate. Michigan also thrives on tourism. People from all over the world visit Michigan's museums and historic sites. They also enjoy winter sports such as skiing and summer sports such as swimming and boating.

While lumber was once a huge industry in Michigan, today it just helps service the paper and furniture-manufacturing industries. Some trees that are harvested include pine, spruce, and hemlock. The area around Escanaba on the Upper Peninsula is a big source of birdseye maple.

Michigan has a wide variety of mineral resources. They include limestone, cement, iron ore, petroleum, natural gas, salt, and gypsum. It also leads the nation in the production of magnesium compounds. Beginning in the 1840s, copper mining was a prime industry in Michigan. But such mining has since ceased. In 1969, a large oil and natural gas field was discovered in the Lower Peninsula. In 2004, it produced 6 million barrels of crude petroleum and 265 billion cubic feet (7.5 billion cu m) of natural gas. While natural

WORDS TO KNOW

exhaust system *the system by which gases leave an automobile*

emissions *substances that are discharged by an automobile*

gas production has continued to increase, the amount of oil being pumped is markedly less than in the mid-1980s.

MINI-BIO

OSAMA SIBLANI: VOICE FOR ARAB AMERICANS

Osama Siblani (1955–), who was born in Beirut, Lebanon, is the publisher of *The Arab American News*, published in Dearborn, Michigan. He moved to the United States in 1976 and graduated from the University of Detroit in 1979. After Israel invaded Lebanon in 1982, he was concerned about how the Middle East was portrayed in the news. He decided to start his own newspaper, which he founded in 1984. In the 20-plus years since, Siblani has earned a reputation for being an intelligent and fair interviewer. His paper is a key source for Arab American information.

Want to know more? See www.arabamericannews.com

BOUNTY FROM MICHIGAN FARMLANDS

If the last salad you ate included cucumbers, they may have come from Michigan. In fact, the state is the national leader in cucumber production. Other salad ingredients from Michigan include, asparagus, carrots, celery, cauliflower, tomatoes, and onions. And if you've recently had a dessert with a cherry on top, the cherry may have come from Michigan, too. The state leads the nation in the production of tart cherries. It is also a major producer of sweet cherries, apples, grapes, peaches, plums, and strawberries. Other core crops include navy beans, corn, soybeans, and wheat. Dairy items are the state's leading agricultural products, and Michigan also raises beef cattle, hogs, and chickens.

In 2005, there were 53,200 farms in Michigan. And these farms covered 10.1 million acres (4.1 million ha). Most of the agricultural activity takes place in the Lower Peninsula. Orchards and vegetable farms are concentrated in a section that runs along Lake Michigan from the Indiana border northward to Grand Traverse Bay and Charlevoix.

Q8 WHAT MICHIGAN TOWN RAISES BULBS FOR TULIPS?

A8 Why, Holland, of course! Dutch settlers founded this community in 1846. And they brought their beautiful flowers with them. The bulbs produce flowers in a rainbow of colors.

Sea lampreys

MINI-BIO

LIZABETH ARDISANA: BRAIN FOR BUSINESS

Lizabeth Ardisana (1951–) spent a year on the European auto racing circuit. But when she settled into a "regular" job, she began working as an engineer for the Ford Motor Company. She later cofounded ASG Renaissance, an international firm headquartered in Dearborn. The company provides marketing and consulting services for a variety of other firms, including Ford.

Ardisana serves on the board of directors for Focus: HOPE, a civil and human rights group dedicated to overcoming poverty, racism, and injustice. And as a Kettering University trustee, she helps recruit students into the engineering field. Ardisana was elected chairperson of the Michigan Hispanic Chamber of Commerce in 2003. She is the first woman to hold that post.

Want to know more? See www.diversitycareers.com/articles/pro/06-junjul/att_liz.htm

GONE FISHING

In the late 1930s, the sea lamprey invaded the Great Lakes. This eel-like fish is a parasite, an animal that relies on other animals to exist, but hurts them in the process. The sea lamprey had nearly wiped out commercial fishing in Michigan. After much research, the U.S. Fish and Wildlife Service found a poison that did away with the lamprey without hurting other fish. So today, Michigan fishers can again catch whitefish, salmon, lake trout, chub, yellow perch, catfish, and carp. Sport fishing is more common than commercial fishing on most of the Great Lakes.

MICHIGAN IN THE AIR

You know that Michigan loves cars. But did you also know that Michiganians helped planes get off the ground? For instance, Harriet Quimby of Branch County was the first American female licensed pilot. She was also the first woman to fly solo across the English Channel.

William Stout founded the Stout Metal Airplane Company in the early 1920s. He built the 2-AT, a single-engine plane used for transporting materials from Dearborn to Chicago. Soon the Ford Motor Company, one of his investors, bought him out. Ford built a three-engine plane called the Tri-Motor, which was used by a number of airlines. But the Ford Motor Company stopped building planes during the Great Depression.

Nancy Harkness Love of Houghton started a flight school at Vassar College in New York, as well as flight clubs all over the country. During World War II, she created the Women's Auxiliary Ferrying Squadron (later called the Women's Air Force Service Pilots). This group transported military supplies throughout the United States.

Two men who were born in Detroit had a huge impact on the flight industry. William Boeing founded the Boeing Airplane Company, a leader in airplane manufacturing, and Charles Lindbergh was the first person to fly nonstop across the Atlantic Ocean.

Harriet Quimby prepares for takeoff in her monoplane in 1912.

Passengers on a car ferry on Lake Michigan watch the sun break out of the fog.

GETTING AROUND

Michigan was a pioneer in urban highway construction and boasts extensive free expressways. As of 2004, there were 122,382 miles (196,954 km) of public highways within the state. And 1,243 miles (2,000 km) of those were interstate highways.

Need to get across one of the Great Lakes? Not to worry—ferries will take you, with or without a car. And you can take a tunnel between Detroit and Windsor, Ontario. Bridges link Michigan with Canada at Sault Sainte Marie, Detroit, and Port Huron. And at Mackinaw City, the Mackinac Bridge links the two peninsulas.

There isn't as much railroad track in Michigan as there used to be. But that's true in most states. These days in Michigan, railroads mostly transport iron ore and other raw materials, as well as new cars and parts for Michigan's many industries. Instead of traveling by train, most people use airplanes for long trips. Michigan has 13 public and private airports. The biggest ones are in Detroit and Grand Rapids.

The Great Lakes are crucial for Michigan's economy. Most of the shipments in and out of Michigan's ports contain materials such as iron, coal, and limestone. Of all the Great Lakes ports, Detroit is the leader. Other key ports are Escanaba, Marquette, Muskegon, and Bay City.

LOOKING FORWARD

In recent decades, the Michigan economy has become less reliant on automobile manufacturing. The service industry has increased. The state saw economic gains in the 1990s. But in the past several years, Michigan has faced a number of problems. Personal income for Michiganians has declined, which means the government has collected less tax income and isn't able to provide as many services. Many cities have seen their populations dwindle, so businesses have closed. But Michiganians are brainstorming new ideas to rejuvenate their economy.

MINI-BIO

SAMUEL C. C. TING: NOTABLE RESEARCHER

Samuel C. C. Ting (1936–) was born in Ann Arbor during the time his parents were attending the University of Michigan. He grew up in China but returned to the United States to attend the University of Michigan. There he earned bachelor's degrees in mathematics and physics in 1959. Three years later, he completed his doctorate in physics. He later became a professor at the Massachusetts Institute of Technology. Throughout his career, he has done groundbreaking research in the field of nuclear energy. He was awarded the Nobel Prize in Physics in 1976.

Want to know more? See www.research.umich.edu/news/michigangreats/ting.html

A ship moving through the Soo Locks on the St. Marys River

CANADA
MINN.
Isle Royale National Park
LAKE SUPERIOR
N
W
E
S
0
50 Miles
0
50 Kilometers
Copper Harbor
Hancock
Houghton
Sault Ste. Marie
CANADA
Marquette
28
Munising
Negaunee
28
2
Iron River
2
75
WISCONSIN
St. Ignace
Mackinac Island
Escanaba
Manistique
Iron Mountain
Menominee
Mackinaw City
Cheboygan
LAKE HURON
Petoskey
Charlevoix
Alpena
75
Interstate highway
28
Other highway
Menominee
Traverse City
Au Sable
Grayling
Oscoda
Manistee
Geographic Center of Michigan
Cadillac
Houghton Lake
Saginaw Bay
75
Ludington
131
Muskegon
WISCONSIN
Big Rapids
Midland
Cass
LAKE MICHIGAN
31
Mount Pleasant
Bay City
Saginaw
Shiawassee
Muskegon
Grand Rapids
Flint
Port Huron
Grand Haven
69
Sterling Heights
96
94
Holland
Lansing
96
Pontiac
196
Battle Creek
Grand
Dearborn
Warren
Kalamazoo
94
Detroit
Benton Harbor
Portage
Ann Arbor
CANADA
ILLINOIS
69
Monroe
LAKE ERIE
94
Niles
Sturgis
Adrian
75
INDIANA
OHIO

CHAPTER NINE

TRAVEL GUIDE

TRAVEL GUIDE

★

WITH ITS GLISTENING WATERFALLS, STUNNING MOUNTAINS, AND MODERN CITIES, THE GREAT LAKES STATE HAS MUCH TO OFFER. Take a trip to automobile-free Mackinac Island. Hike through the Upper Peninsula region, where parks and lighthouses are abundant. For the urban experience, head to the Motor City, Detroit.

← Follow along with this travel map. We'll begin in Sault Sainte Marie and travel all the way down to Detroit!

UPPER PENINSULA REGION

THINGS TO DO: Hike through a park, learn about lightkeepers, or visit Sault Sainte Marie, Michigan's oldest town.

Sault Sainte Marie

★ **Soo Locks:** Experience the engineering marvel of the Soo Locks. Numerous displays inside the center chronicle the construction and the people who made the locks possible. A 30-minute movie provides an explanation of the need for and use of this maritime wonder.

SEE IT HERE!

GREAT LAKES SHIPWRECK MUSEUM

Have you ever heard of the *Edmund Fitzgerald*? On November 10, 1975, this ship was sailing on Lake Superior when it mysteriously disappeared. The vessel and its 29-man crew were lost forever.

You can learn about this dramatic story and many others at the Great Lakes Shipwreck Museum at Whitefish Point. It is located at the site of the oldest active lighthouse on Lake Superior. Want to know more? See www.shipwreckmuseum.com

Point Iroquois Light Station

★ **Point Iroquois Light Station:** Located just outside of Sault Sainte Marie, this museum reveals the stories of the Point Iroquois lightkeepers and their families through family photographs, antiques, and artifacts.

★ **Tower of History:** Soaring 210 feet (64 m) above Sault Sainte Marie and the Soo Locks, the tower has observation platforms for visitors to get spectacular views and photos of the world's busiest inland shipping channel.

Marquette

★ **Marquette Maritime Museum:** This museum tells the fascinating story of the maritime heritage of Marquette and Lake Superior. Exhibits include birch bark canoes and a lighthouse lens.

★ **U.S. National Ski Hall of Fame and Museum:** Located a few miles outside of Marquette, in Ishpeming, this museum honors the men and women who have enriched the sport.

★ **Michigan Iron Industry Museum:** This museum overlooks the Carp River and the site of the first iron forge in the Lake Superior region. It features exhibits, audio-visual programs, and outdoor trails.

Escanaba

★ **U.P. Steam & Gas Engine Museum:** Here you'll see steam-powered tractors and other agricultural equipment, as well as working steam and gas engines.

SEE IT HERE!

ISLE ROYALE NATIONAL PARK

This national park is made up of Isle Royale, the largest island in Lake Superior, and about 200 tiny islands. This park has no roads and teems with wildlife, including moose and wolves. It's a great place to enjoy nature hikes.

Iron Mountain

★ **House of Yesteryear Museum:** This is a collection of 30 cars in mint condition that were made between 1910 and 1939. The museum also features a collection of 179 guns and 50 skates, 435 license plates, fire engines, tractors, clothing, and homemaking artifacts.

Keweenaw Peninsula

★ **Keweenaw National Historical Park:** This beautiful national historical park celebrates the region's copper-mining heritage, which dates back 7,000 years. Learn about how Native peoples made copper into tools and trade items, how investors and immigrants arrived in the 1800s in a great mineral rush, and how developing industries and communities built up the region.

G.R.C. Library

MACKINAC ISLAND REGION

THINGS TO DO: Explore a historic fort, enjoy the hustle and bustle of downtown Mackinac Island, and take a carriage ride!

Mackinac Island

★ **Mackinac Island State Park:** This park dates back to 1895 and boasts dense stands of cedars and birches, along with limestone bluffs that tower over wildflowers and crystal waters. On your visit, you might get around on bicycles and horse-drawn carriages because cars are not allowed on the island.

★ **Mackinac Island's Historic Downtown District:** You'll see 19th-century life re-created on Market and Huron streets in the Biddle House, Benjamin blacksmith shop, Dr. Beaumont Museum, McGulpin House, Indian dormitory, and mission church. Historic reenactors (people who pretend they're from the period) stitch quilts, cook meals over fires, and provide insight into the lives of Mackinac Island's early settlers. Don't miss the shops that sell homemade fudge.

Arch Rock on Mackinac Island

★ **Fort Mackinac:** Tour Michigan's oldest buildings and imagine what life was like in this 200-year-old fortress.

★ **Surrey Hill Square Carriage Museum:** Enjoy an antique carriage museum with a working blacksmith shop.

NORTHEAST REGION

THINGS TO DO: Enjoy cross-country skiing and snowmobile rides, craft shows and concerts in the park, and museums and lighthouses.

Cheboygan

★ **Cheboygan Opera House:** See one of northern Michigan's premiere music halls. It offers a concert series, shows classic films, and holds theater workshops.

★ **Cheboygan County Historical Museum Complex**: Explore the rich history of the Cheboygan area at the Cheboygan County Historical Museum Complex. The buildings include a settlers' log cabin, originally located on Burt Lake in a local Indian village, and the Cheboygan County sheriff residence constructed in 1882.

★ **Cheboygan Crib Light:** It once toppled into the Cheboygan River, but this 25-foot (8m) steel tower was pulled ashore and restored. It is now located at the mouth of the Cheboygan River, on the banks of Lake Huron, at the Doyle Recreation Area.

Oscoda

★ **Au Sable-Oscoda Historical Society & Museum:** Here you can learn about Indian artifacts and treaties, early commercial fishing, shipping and local shipwrecks, the booming logging industry, the 1911 fire that destroyed the two towns, and the history of Wurtsmith Air Force Base.

★ **Lumberman's Monument Visitor Center:** Since 1932, this huge bronze memorial to Michigan's lumbering era has sat on a high bluff overlooking the sparkling waters of the Au Sable River. Interpretive signs and exhibits tell the story of moving logs from the forests to the mills. Enjoy climbing the logjam and using the crosscut saw.

★ **Yankee Air Museum:** This division of the main museum in Ypsilanti is located at the Willow Run Airport. You'll see both flyable and grounded aircraft, artifacts and equipment, memorabilia, and a library for research and public information.

Grayling

★ **The Bottle-Cap Museum:** More than 9,000 pieces of memorabilia make up the museum, which is housed in the authentic Dawson and Stevens Classic 50s Diner located in downtown Grayling.

The Bottle-Cap Museum

★ **Hartwick Pines Logging Museum:** At this museum, you'll return to the 19th-century logging era, when thousands of men cut millions of board feet of lumber.

Houghton

★ **Houghton Lake:** Enjoy canoeing, kayaking, fishing, golfing, jet skiing, swimming, and hiking. Or read a good book while sitting by the lake.

NORTHWEST REGION

THINGS TO DO: Stop by the Cherry Capital of the World, or enjoy quaint little towns and historic sites.

Mackinaw City

★ **Colonial Michilimackinac State Historic Park:** In 1770, Michilimackinac was the first stop for voyagers, and it still is. A fiddler leads you on a tour of the grounds.

★ **Mill Creek State Historic Park:** As the Straits of Mackinac's first industrial complex, Mill Creek provided sawn lumber for the settlement of Mackinac Island in the 1790s. Today at Mill Creek, you can see chipmunks, watch hawks, smell the cedars, or take the end of a big saw to help cut in the saw pit.

SEE IT HERE!

SLEEPING BEAR DUNES NATIONAL LAKESHORE

When you visit Sleeping Bear Dunes National Lakeshore, you can enjoy the Pierce Stocking Scenic Drive , which snakes through the park for 7 miles (11 km) and offers spectacular overlooks. You can explore the Manitou Islands. And, of course, you can climb the dunes! This park, located near Empire, has 35 miles (56 km) of coastline.

Traverse City

★ **Grand Traverse Heritage Center:** See the Con Foster Collection featured in new galleries, which includes artifacts from Native American cultures and railroad history, along with a blacksmith shop, a one-room school, and an old-time parlor.

A pie-eating contestant at the National Cherry Festival

★ **National Cherry Festival:** Traverse City is known as the Cherry Capital of the World. Enjoy cherry pie and cherry picking at the National Cherry Festival, held every July.

★ **World's Biggest Cherry Pie Tin:** This tin was entered into the *Guinness Book of World Records* after it held a 28,350-pound (12,859 kg) cherry pie that was 17 feet, 6 inches (5.3 m) in diameter!

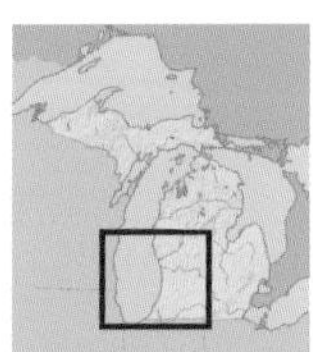

SOUTHWEST REGION

THINGS TO DO: Learn about naval history, spend time on a sunny beach, take in a historic mansion, or visit an outdoor sculpture collection.

Muskegon

★ **Fire Barn Museum and Exhibit:** This 1870s firehouse is now a site of the Muskegon County Museum and serves as a living memorial to the brave men and women who have served as Muskegon County firefighters.

★ **Great Lakes Naval Memorial and Museum:** Step back in time and tour a World War II submarine, the USS *Silversides*, and a 1920s Coast Guard cutter, the USCGC *McLane*.

★ **Hackley and Hume Historic Site:** These two restored Queen Anne–style houses, built in the late 1880s, were the homes of two of Muskegon's most prominent lumber barons. They feature intricate wood carvings, stained glass, stenciled walls and ceilings, some original furniture, and family possessions.

SEE IT HERE!

HURON-MANISTEE NATIONAL FORESTS

Want to go hiking, camping, or canoeing? Then you might enjoy two areas of forest that spread across the Lower Peninsula. The Huron-Manistee National Forests spread across more than 976,000 acres (395,000 ha) and provide a great place for animals and plants to live—and for people to play! The Huron National Forest was established in 1909. The Manistee National Forest was established in 1938. In 1945, the administration of the two areas was combined. While you are in the forests, you might see white-tailed deer, coyotes, raccoons, and maybe even black bears!

Grand Rapids

★ **Gerald R. Ford Presidential Museum:** Diverse exhibits show the real stuff of history at this museum. Learn about Ford's days in the White House and his influence on the nation and the world.

Space program statue outside the Gerald R. Ford Presidential Museum

★ **Van Andel Museum Center of the Public Museum of Grand Rapids:** This world-class education and entertainment center includes an operating 1928 carousel and the Roger B. Chaffee Planetarium, which is equipped with a digital sound system, and multiple video projectors capable of numerous special effects.

★ **Voigt House Victorian Museum:** Dating back to 1895, this home contains original furnishings, personal items, and clothing of the Voigt family, who built it and occupied it for 76 years.

★ **Frederik Meijer Gardens and Sculpture Park:** This botanic garden and sculpture park boasts a butterfly garden, a tropical conservatory, and a carnivorous (meat-eating) plant house. One treasure at the park is *The American Horse*, a sculpture that is 24 feet (7.3 m) tall.

Grand Haven

★ **Depot Museum:** The Depot Museum, situated on the banks of the Grand River in the former Grand Trunk Railroad depot, provides a glimpse into Michigan's nautical heritage.

★ **Tri-Cities Historical Museum:** The Tri-Cities Historical Museum provides visitors with an opportunity to look through the windows of time into the history of northwest Ottawa County, including the communities of Grand Haven, Spring Lake, and Ferrysburg.

Holland

★ **Dutch Village:** A Dutch heritage theme park with more than 10 acres (4 ha) of 19th-century Netherlands village life. Visit a re-creation of a 100-year-old Dutch town featuring folk dancers, wooden shoe carving, museums, a movie, a farmhouse, and rides. And you can't miss the tulips!

Dancers at the Tulip Festival in Holland

★ **Holland Museum:** Enjoy Holland's heritage at three museum sites: the Holland Museum, the Cappon House, and the Settlers House. All three sites are listed on the National Register of Historic Places.

Kalamazoo

★ **Air Zoo:** At this aviation museum that celebrates the Wright brothers' first flight, you can take a virtual tour of the International Space Station or take the controls of a military jet plane.

★ **Kalamazoo Valley Museum:** This is a museum of history and technology linking southwestern Michigan to the world through exhibits, programs, a planetarium, and a learning center. Visitors can view cultural and scientific artifacts and experience a simulated space flight.

SEE IT HERE!

FRANKENMUTH

Frankenmuth may be known as Little Bavaria, after the region in Germany, but it is located right in Saginaw Valley. While you are there, you can try all kinds of German food, from sausages to sauerkraut. More than 3 million people visit Frankenmuth each year.

SOUTHEAST REGION

THINGS TO DO: Visit the historic capital of Lansing, tour the University of Michigan campus, or take in the metropolitan excitement of Detroit.

Lansing

★ **All Around the African World Museum:** This museum celebrates the history of and contributions by people of African descent all around the world.

★ **Michigan Historical Museum:** At this museum, you can walk through an Upper Peninsula copper mine, stroll along a 1920s street, or explore the 1957 Detroit Auto Show.

Kitchen exhibit at the Michigan Historical Museum

★ **Michigan Women's Historical Center and Hall of Fame:** This center houses the Michigan Women's Hall of Fame gallery and the Belen Art Gallery, which displays the work of female artists and photographers from Michigan.

★ **R.E. Olds Transportation Museum:** This museum features artifacts and documents tracing the history of area transportation from 1883 to the present. Antique vehicles and automotive memorabilia, as well as aircraft, bicycles, and carriages, are displayed.

★ **Michigan State University:** Visit the beautiful campus of Michigan State University. Be sure to catch a Spartans basketball game or tour the Michigan State University Athletics Hall of Fame, which features athletes such as Magic Johnson and Kirk Gibson.

★ **Michigan State Capitol:** Explore the historic hallways of the state capitol, where decisions about Michigan are made every day.

Dearborn

★ **The Henry Ford:** This indoor-outdoor American history museum (also known as the Henry Ford Museum and Greenfield Village) is the most popular tourist attraction in Michigan. While you are there, you can ride a Model T and view incredible artifacts such as the chair in which Abraham Lincoln was sitting when he was shot, John F. Kennedy's limousine, and the Wright Brothers' bicycle shop.

★ **Automotive Hall of Fame:** At this site, you can learn all about the history of the automobile business and the men and women who made important contributions to it.

MINI-BIO

ALBERT KAHN: MASTER BUILDER

Who designed all those factories in Michigan? Many were the vision of Albert Kahn (1869–1942). Known as the best industrial architect of his time, Kahn designed the Packard Motor Company plant in 1907. In his style of construction, Kahn used reinforced concrete for walls, supports, and roofs. Using concrete instead of wood allowed him to make the buildings more fireproof and the rooms big and open. He went on to design Ford's Highland Park and River Rouge plants. But he didn't design only factories. Kahn designed the art deco Fisher Building in Detroit and the Dearborn Inn, the first airport hotel in the world.

Want to know more? See www.si.umich.edu/umarch/architects/kahn.html

WOW

Detroit is the only major city in the continental United States that lies north of the Canadian border.

★ **The Ford River Rouge Factory Tour:** Go behind the scenes inside the world's largest automotive complex. You'll see assembly lines and other manufacturing marvels. You can even view where Ford F-150 light trucks are made.

Detroit

★ **Detroit Historical Museum:** Exhibits present the history of southeastern Michigan, including the newly renovated Streets of Old Detroit, and re-creations of Detroit street scenes from the 1840s, 1870s, and early 1900s.

★ **Detroit Zoo:** Located in the suburb of Royal Oak, this zoo opened in 1928. It boasts exhibits of tigers, polar bears, and many other creatures, and is known for aiding threatened animals. It helped reintroduce trumpeter swans to the wild, and it has taken in abused circus animals. Today, it features a wide variety of animals from around the world. The zoo is managed by the Detroit Zoological Society, which also oversees the Belle Isle Nature Zoo.

Tiger cub

WRITING PROJECTS

Check out these ideas for creating election brochures and writing you-are-there editorials. Or learn about the state quarter and design your own.

118

ART PROJECTS

Make your own dream catcher, illustrate the state song, or create a great PowerPoint presentation.

119

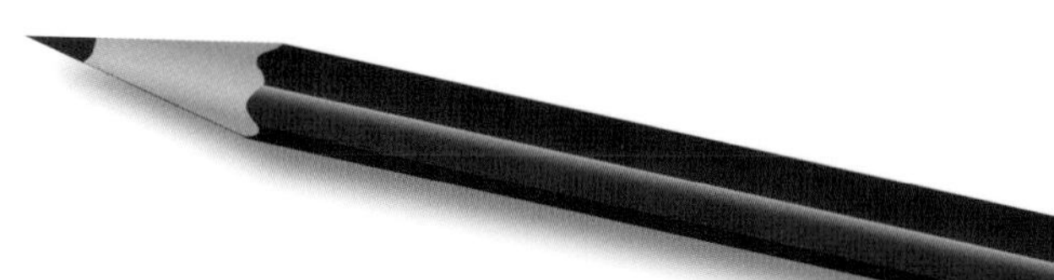

TIMELINE

What happened when? This timeline highlights important events in the state's history—and shows what was happening throughout the United States at the same time.

122

FAST FACTS

Use this section to find fascinating facts about state symbols, land area and population statistics, weather, sports teams, and much more.

126

GLOSSARY

Remember the Words to Know from the chapters in this book? They're all collected here.

125

SCIENCE, TECHNOLOGY, & MATH PROJECTS

Make weather maps, graph population statistics, or research endangered species that live in the state.

120

PRIMARY VS. SECONDARY SOURCES

121

So what are primary and secondary sources, and what's the diff? This section explains all that and where you can find them.

BIOGRAPHICAL DICTIONARY

133

This at-a-glance guide highlights some of the state's most important and influential people. You can read about their contributions to the state, the country, and the world.

RESOURCES

Books, Web sites, DVDs, and more. Take a look at these additional sources for information about the state.

137

WRITING PROJECTS

★ ★ ★

Write a Memoir, Journal, or Editorial For Your School Newspaper

Picture Yourself . . .

★ as a member of the Huron, Ojibwa, Odawa, or Potawatomi during Michigan's early days. Compose journal entries about everyday life. Describe what it was like when European explorers arrived in your village.

SEE: Chapter Two, pages 22–25.

★ as a participant in the civil rights movement. Consider what it would have been like to work for equal rights with Martin Luther King Jr. Keep a journal of your experiences, including the speeches you heard and the resistance you encountered. What kept you going?

SEE: Chapters Four and Five, pages 43–46, 56–58.

GO TO: The NAACP (National Association for the Advancement of Colored People) Web site at www.naacp.org to find out more.

Create an Election Brochure or Web Site

Run for office!

Pretend you are a candidate for governor of Michigan and create a campaign brochure or Web site. Explain how you meet the qualifications for governor and talk about the three or four major issues you'll focus on if you are elected. Remember, you'll be responsible for Michigan's budget. How do you propose to spend the taxpayers' money?

SEE: Chapter Seven, pages 80–81.

GO TO: Michigan's government Web site at www.michigan.gov.

Research Mighigan's State Quarter

From 1999 to 2008, the U.S. Mint introduced new quarters commemorating each of the 50 states in the order that they were admitted into the Union. Each state's quarter features a unique design on its reverse, or back.

GO TO: www.usmint.gov/kids and find out what's featured on the back of the Michigan quarter.

Research and write an essay explaining:

★ the significance of each image.

★ who designed the quarter.

★ who chose the final design.

Design your own Michigan state quarter. What images would you choose for the reverse?

★ Make a poster showing the Michigan quarter and label each image.

ART PROJECTS

★ ★ ★

Create a PowerPoint Presentation or Visitors' Guide

Welcome to Michigan! Michigan is a great place to visit—and to live! From its natural beauty to its bustling cities and historic sites, there's plenty to see and do. In your PowerPoint presentation or brochure, highlight 10 to 15 of Michigan's fascinating landmarks. Be sure to include:

★ a map of the state locating these sites.

★ photos, illustrations, Web links, natural history facts, geographic stats, climate and weather, and plants and wildlife.

SEE: Chapter One, pages 9–19, and Chapter Nine, pages 104–115.

GO TO: The Web sites of Michigan tourism at www.enjoyMichigan.com and www.michigan.org/travel/. Download and print maps, photos, national landmark images, and vacationing ideas.

Illustrate the Lyrics to the Michigan State Song ("My Michigan")

Use markers, paints, photos, collages, colored pencils, or computer graphics to illustrate the lyrics to "My Michigan," the state song. Turn your illustrations into a picture book, or scan them into a PowerPoint presentation and add music.

SEE: The lyrics to "My Michigan" on page 128.

GO TO: The Michigan state Web site at www.michigan.gov to find out more about the origin of the state song.

Catch a Dream with Your Own Ojibwa Dream Catcher!

★ Study the history, myth, and lore behind the Native American dream catcher.

★ Research early models of dream catchers and their cultural value to the Michigan Ojibwa.

★ Using various art supplies, create your own Native American dream catcher. Create the dream catcher as an embodiment of your personality, spirituality, and dreams.

SEE: Chapter Two, page 24.

GO TO: www.nativetech.org/dreamcat/dreminst.html for instructions.

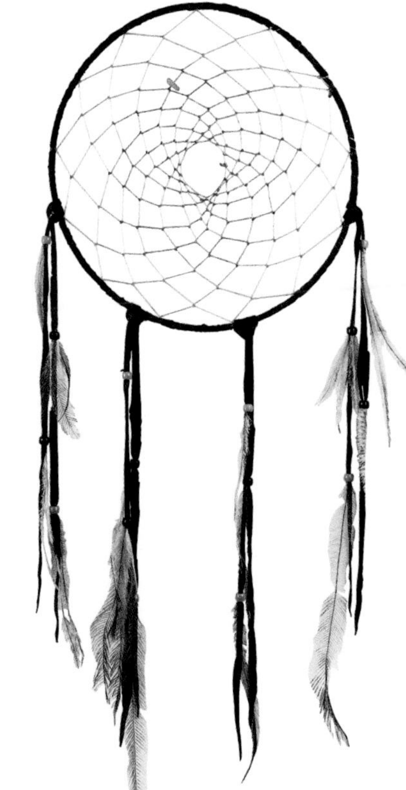

Dream catcher

SCIENCE, TECHNOLOGY, & MATH PROJECTS

★ ★ ★

Graph Population Statistics!

- ★ Compare population statistics (such as ethnic background, birth, death, and literacy rates) in Michigan counties or major cities.
- ★ Look at population densities, and write sentences describing what the population statistics show; graph one set of population statistics, write a paragraph explaining what the graphs reveal.

SEE: Chapter Six, pages 64–66.

GO TO: The official Web site for the U.S. Census Bureau at www.census.gov, and at quickfacts.census.gov/qfd/states/26000.html, to find out more about population statistics, how they work, and what the statistics are for Michigan.

Create a Weather Map of Michigan!

Use your knowledge of Michigan's geography to research and identify conditions that result in specific weather events. How does the geography of Michigan make it vulnerable to things such as blizzards? Create a weather map or poster that shows the state's weather patterns. To accompany your map, explain the technology used to measure weather phenomena.

SEE: Chapter One, pages 14–15.

GO TO: The National Oceanic and Atmospheric Administration's National Weather Service Web site at www.weather.gov for weather maps and forecasts for Michigan.

Track Endangered Species

Using your knowledge of Michigan's wildlife, research what animals and plants are endangered or threatened. Find out what the state is doing to protect these species. Chart known populations of the animals and plants and report on changes in certain geographic areas.

SEE: Chapter One, page 17.

GO TO: The U.S. Fish and Wildlife site at www.fws.gov/Midwest/endangered/lists/state-mi.html or other Michigan-specific sites such as www.endangeredspecie.com/states/mi.htm

Gray wolves

PRIMARY VS. SECONDARY SOURCES

★ ★ ★

What's the Diff?

Your teacher may require at least one or two primary sources and one or two secondary sources for your assignment. So, what's the difference between the two?

- **Primary sources are original.** You are reading the actual words of someone's diary, journal, letter, autobiography, or interview. Primary sources can also be photographs, maps, prints, cartoons, news/film footage, posters, first-person newspaper articles, drawings, musical scores, and recordings. By the way, when you conduct a survey, interview someone, shoot a video, or take photographs to include in a project, you are creating primary sources!
- **Secondary sources are what you find in encyclopedias, textbooks, articles, biographies, and almanacs.** These are written by a person or group of people who tell about something that happened to someone else. Secondary sources also recount what another person said or did. This book is an example of a secondary source.

Now that you know what primary sources are—where can you find them?

- **Your school or local library:** Check the library catalog for collections of original writings, government documents, musical scores, and so on. Some of this material may be stored on microfilm. The Library of Congress Web site (www.loc.gov) is an excellent online resource for primary source materials.
- **Historical societies:** These organizations keep historical documents, photographs, and other materials. Staff members can help you find what you are looking for. History museums are also great places to see primary sources firsthand.
- **The Internet:** There are lots of sites that have primary sources you can download and use in a project or assignment.

TIMELINE

★ ★ ★

U.S. Events

1619
The first African indentured laborers in English North America are purchased for work in the Jamestown settlement.

1754–63
England and France fight over North American colonial lands in the French and Indian War. By the end of the war, France has ceded all of its land west of the Mississippi to Spain and its Canadian territories to England.

1787
The U.S. Constitution is written.

1803
The Louisiana Purchase almost doubles the size of the United States.

1600

Michigan Events

1618
Étienne Brûlé reaches Sault Sainte Marie.

1668
Jacques Marquette founds the first permanent European settlement in Michigan.

Jacques Marquette

1700

1701
Antoine de la Mothe, sieur de Cadillac, establishes Fort Pontchartrain.

1715
The French set up Fort Michilimackinac at the Straits of Mackinac.

1760
The French surrender Fort Pontchartrain to the British, ending French rule in Detroit.

1763
Pontiac's Rebellion takes place.

1783
The Treaty of Paris is signed.

1796
The U.S. flag is raised over Detroit when the British finally leave the city.

1800

1805
Michigan Territory is created, with William Hull as governor.

U.S. Events

Michigan Events

1812
Detroit and Fort Mackinac are surrendered to the British during the War of 1812.

1813
The Battle of River Raisin is fought; American forces reenter Detroit.

1819
The Treaty of Saginaw cedes nearly 6 million acres (2.4 million ha) of Indian lands to Michigan settlers.

The Erie Canal

1825
The Erie Canal opens.

1828
The territorial capitol is built at Detroit.

1830
The Indian Removal Act forces eastern Native American groups to relocate west of the Mississippi River.

1837
Michigan becomes a state on January 26.

1846–48
The United States engages in a war with Mexico over western territories in the Mexican War.

1847
The legislature passes a law to make Lansing the state capital.

1852
Michigan's first labor union is formed.

1861–65
The American Civil War is fought between the Northern Union and the Southern Confederacy.

1861
The First Michigan Infantry enters the Civil War.

1900

1908
Ford begins manufacturing the Model T.

1917
Michiganians begin fighting in World War I.

1929
The stock market crashes, plunging the United States more deeply into the Great Depression.

U.S. Events

1941–45
The United States engages in World War II.

Martin Luther King Jr.

1964–73
The United States engages in the Vietnam War.

1991
The United States and other nations fight the brief Persian Gulf War against Iraq.

2000

2001
Terrorists hijack four U.S. aircraft and crash them into the World Trade Center in New York City, the Pentagon in Washington, D.C., and a Pennsylvania field, killing thousands.

2003
The United States and coalition forces invade Iraq.

Michigan Events

1932
A protest march at Ford's River Rouge Plant turns violent.

1941
After the attack on Pearl Harbor, Michiganians engage in World War II.

1957
The Mackinac Bridge opens.

1959
Berry Gordy founds Motown Records in Detroit.

1963
Martin Luther King Jr. leads the Great March to Freedom.

1967
Race riots break out in Detroit and other cities.

1974
Gerald Ford becomes the 38th president of the United States.

1977
The Renaissance Center is built in Detroit.

1980s
Michigan endures a recession.

2002
Jennifer M. Granholm is elected Michigan's first female governor.

2007
The Auto Workers Union goes on strike for two days over job security.

GLOSSARY

alliance an association between groups that benefits all the members

circuit courts courts that are located at two or more places in one judicial district

civil rights the rights of personal liberty that are guaranteed to all citizens

convert to bring a person over from one opinion or belief to another

discrimination the act of treating people unfairly because of their race or other classification

documentary something that is factual and shows real life

firebreaks barriers of cleared land created as a way to stop forest fires from spreading

fugitives people who flee or try to escape

emissions substances that are discharged by an automobile

exhaust system the system by which gases leave an automobile

lubricating making smooth or slippery as a way to reduce friction and heat

mediator someone who helps others settle their differences

mission a place created by a religious group to spread its beliefs

peninsula a body of land surrounded by water on three sides but connected to a larger piece of land

poll taxes fees that people must pay before they can vote

recessions periods of reduced economic activity

riot public disorder or violence

siege a military blockade (the closing down of a city or fort to outside people and supplies), usually used to make a group surrender

sit-down strike a refusal to work, while remaining at the place of employment

straits narrow passageways of water that connect larger bodies of water

temperate marked by moderation; mild

treaty an agreement between two or more groups, often to end a conflict

veto to reject a proposed law

FAST FACTS

State Symbols

State seal

Statehood date January 26, 1837, the 26th state

Origin of state name From the Ojibwa word *michigama*, meaning "great lake"

State capital Lansing

State nickname Wolverine State, Great Lakes State, Water Wonderland

State motto *Si quaeris peninsulam amoenam circumspice* ("If you seek a pleasant peninsula, look about you")

State bird Robin

State flower Apple blossom

State fish Brook trout

State rock Petoskey stone

State gem Chlorastrolite (Isle Royale greenstone)

State song "My Michigan" (See lyrics on page 128)

State tree White pine

State fair Escanaba for the Upper Peninsula (mid-August) Detroit for the Lower Peninsula (late August or early September)

State flag

Geography

Total area; rank 96,716 square miles (250,494 sq km); 11th

Land; rank 56,804 square miles (147,122 sq km); 22nd

Water; rank 39,912 square miles (103,372 sq km); 2nd

Inland water; rank 1,611 square miles (4,172 sq km); 13th

Great Lakes; rank 38,301 square miles (99,200 sq km); 1st

Geographic center In Wexford County, 5 miles (8 km) northwest of Cadillac

Latitude and Longitude 41° 41′ N to 48° 15′ N
82° 26′ W to 90° 31′ W

Highest point Mount Arvon, 1,979 feet (603 m)

Lowest point 571 feet (174 m) along Lake Erie

Largest city Detroit

Number of counties 83

Longest river Grand River, 260 miles (418 km)

Pine cone

Population

Population; rank (2006 estimate)	10,095,643; 8th
Density (2006 estimate)	178 persons per square mile (69 per sq km)
Population distribution (2000 census)	75% urban, 25% rural
Race (2005 estimate)	White persons: 77.9%*
	Black persons: 14.3%*
	Asian persons: 2.2%*
	American Indian and Alaska Native persons: 0.6%*
	Native Hawaiian and Other Pacific Islander: 0.0%*
	Persons reporting two or more races: 1.5%
	Persons of Hispanic or Latino origin: 3.8%†

** Includes persons reporting only one race.*

† Hispanics may be of any race, so are also included in applicable race categories.

Weather

Record high temperature	112°F (44°C) at Mio on July 13, 1936
Record low temperature	–51°F (–46°C) at Vanderbilt on February 9, 1934
Average January temperature	25°F (–4°C)
Average July temperature	74°F (23°C)
Average yearly precipitation	32.8 inches (83.3 cm)

A snow day in Battle Creek

STATE SONG

"My Michigan"

Words by Giles Kavanagh; Music by by H. O'Reilly Clint

"My Michigan," with lyrics by Giles Kavanagh and music by H. O'Reilly Clint, was named an official state song by the state legislature in 1937. "Michigan, My Michigan!" a more popular song, has long been considered an unofficial state song.

All hail My Michigan, Flower of our Union Great!
Health to My Michigan, From the Upper to the Strait,
And may the wash of your salt-less seas, While the zephyrs gently sway your trees,
Sing to you Michigan! Might in War and Right in Peace.
Hail La Salle, to Cadillac of old, To ev'ry pioneer we pledge their faith to hold.
Oh Michigan! My Michigan! May their noble deeds be ever told.
So All hail my My Michigan, Flower of our Union Great!
Health to My Michigan, From the Upper to the Strait,
And may the wash of your salt-less seas, While the zephyrs gently sway your trees,
Sing to you Michigan! Might in War and Right in Peace.
Three cheers My Michigan, And a lusty Tiger too.
Long live My Michigan With a Will and Heart so true.
From Erie's marshes to Keweenaw May the glory of your grandeur stand.
God bless you Michigan, Fairest state in all our land.
From canoe of birch to motor car, From ev'ry sugar beet and ev'ry copper bar
Your life began My Michigan! To our land you are the guiding Star.
So Three cheers My Michigan, And a lusty Tiger too.
Long live My Michigan With a Will and Heart so true.
From Erie's marshes to Keweenaw May the glory of your grandeur stand.
God bless you Michigan, Fairest state in all our land.
Here's to My Michigan, May your standard never fade!
We love you Michigan, Ev'ry lake and ev'ry glade;
So let our hearts sing in harmony, Let our voices ring in praise of you.
God save you Michigan! We'll defend you, we'll be true.
To the years, the days that are to be We dedicate our lives to Honor, Liberty
For Michigan, My Michigan! Hold the torch of Tuebor loftily.
So Here's to My Michigan, May your standard never fade!
We love you Michigan, Ev'ry lake and ev'ry glade;
So let our hearts sing in harmony, Let our voices ring in praise of you.
God save you Michigan! We'll defend you, we'll be true.

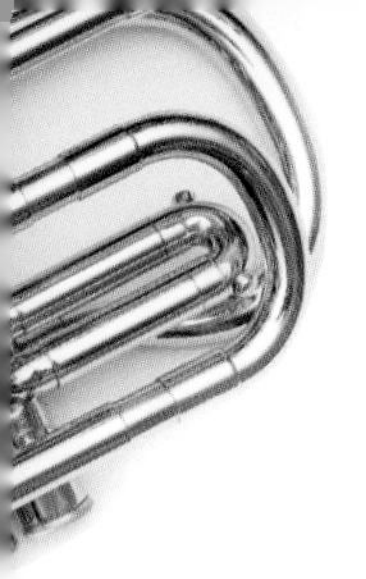

NATIONAL AREAS AND HISTORICAL SITES

★ ★ ★

National Park

Isle Royale National Park comprises more than 200 islands in Lake Superior.

National Lakeshores

Pictured Rocks National Lakeshore, near Munising on Lake Superior, has beautifully colored cliffs carved into wonderful shapes by the waves. This was the first national lakeshore. *Sleeping Bear Dunes National Lakeshore,* near Empire on Lake Michigan, is the only national park area in the Lower Peninsula.

National Historic Park

Keweenaw National Historic Park commemorates the first significant copper mining in the United States.

National Memorial

Father Marquette National Memorial commemorates the French Jesuit missionary's accomplishments.

National Forests

Michigan is home to three national forests: *Ottawa*, *Hiawatha*, and *Huron-Manistee*. Together, they encompass 2.8 million acres (1.1 million ha) in northern Michigan along the Great Lakes.

State Parks

Michigan's park system is one of the largest in the United States. It has 3,900,000 acres (1,600,000 ha) of state forests and game areas, as well as 97 state parks and recreation areas.

Arboretums

Leila Arboretum (Battle Creek) is a landscaped park with rare plants and a wildlife museum. *Nichols Arboretum* (Ann Arbor) is home to more than 600 species of trees and shrubs, including more than 230 kinds of peonies.

Kayaking near Pictured Rocks National Lakeshore

SPORTS TEAMS

★ ★ ★

NCAA Teams (Division I)

Central Michigan University *Chippewas*
Eastern Michigan University *Eagles*
Michigan State University *Spartans*
Oakland University *Golden Grizzlies*
University of Detroit Mercy *Titans*
University of Michigan *Wolverines*
Western Michigan University *Broncos*

PROFESSIONAL SPORTS TEAMS

★ ★ ★

Major League Baseball

Detroit Tigers

National Basketball Association

Detroit Pistons

Women's National Basketball Association

Detroit Shock

National Football League

Detroit Lions

Hockey

Detroit Red Wings

CULTURAL INSTITUTIONS

Libraries

The Detroit Public Library (Detroit) has several collections on Michigan and Great Lakes history.

The Gerald R. Ford Library (Ann Arbor) holds the papers of the former president.

The Library of Michigan (Lansing) is the state library. It has collections of state and federal documents, as well as collections on Michigan genealogy and law.

The Walter P. Reuther Library (Detroit) is at Wayne State University. Its collections on labor history and the Detroit region are invaluable to researchers.

Museums

The Sloan Museum (Flint) features the history of transportation.

The Detroit Historical Museum (Detroit) features artifacts and exhibits on the city's history and people.

The Detroit Institute of Arts (Detroit) has Diego Rivera's great Detroit Industry frescoes and a fine collection of American Art

The Grand Rapids Public Museum (Grand Rapids) features exhibits on natural history.

The Henry Ford Museum and Greenfield Village (Dearborn) is a living history museum with exhibits on industry and life in the 1700s and 1800s.

The Kingman Museum of Natural History (Battle Creek) has exhibits of wildlife, prehistoric mammals, and ancient relics.

The Michigan Historical Museum (Lansing) displays items dating from prehistoric times to the modern industrial era.

National Ski Hall of Fame (Ishpeming) pays tribute to skiing events and people who have made outstanding contributions to the sport.

Performing Arts

Michigan has three major symphony orchestras and two major opera companies.

Universities and Colleges

As of 2007, Michigan had 43 public and 51 independent institutions of higher education.

ANNUAL EVENTS

January–March

Tip-Up Town, U.S.A. (ice-fishing festival) in Houghton Lake (January)

International 500 Snowmobile Race in Sault Sainte Marie (early February)

Tahquamenon Falls Nordic Invitational Ski Race in Newberry (mid-March)

April–June

Maple Syrup Festival in Shepherd and Vermontville (April)

National Trout Festival in Kalkaska (April)

Blossomtime Festival in St. Joseph-Benton Harbor (May)

Highland Festival and Games in Alma (May)

Bavarian Festival in Frankenmuth (June)

Cereal Festival in Battle Creek (June)

National Strawberry Festival in Belleville (June)

International Freedom Festival in Detroit (late June–early July)

July–September

National Cherry Festival in Traverse City (early July)

Ann Arbor Art Fairs (July)

Yacht Races at Mackinac Island from Chicago and Port Huron (July)

October–December

Fall color tours, statewide (October)

Red Flannel Festival in Cedar Springs (October)

Hunting season: parts of Upper and Lower Peninsulas (October–November), statewide (November)

Christmas at Greenfield Village in Dearborn (December)

BIOGRAPHICAL DICTIONARY

Mitch Albom

Mitch Albom (1958–) is a novelist and a sportswriter for the *Detroit Free Press.*

Tim Allen (1953–) is an actor and comedian who grew up in Birmingham and graduated from Western Michigan University. He was born in Colorado.

Lizabeth Ardisana See page 100.

Lois Beardslee See page 25.

William Boeing (1881–1956) founded the Boeing Airplane Company, a leader in airplane manufacturing. He was born in Detroit.

Étienne Brûlé (c. 1592–c. 1633) was a French explorer who was probably the first European to arrive in Michigan. He reached Sault Sainte Marie in 1618.

Ralph Bunche See page 57.

Tim Allen

Antoine de la Mothe Cadillac (1658–1730) was a French explorer who established Fort Pontchartrain in 1701. The site later became the city of Detroit.

Lewis Cass (1782–1866) served as governor of Michigan Territory from 1813 to 1831.

Ty Cobb (1886–1961) was a Hall of Fame baseball star who played for the Detroit Tigers from 1905 to 1921. He was originally from Georgia.

John Conyers Jr. See page 82.

Francis Ford Coppola (1939–) is a renowned film director. He was born in Detroit.

Christopher Paul Curtis (1953–) has written children's books including *The Watsons Go to Birmingham—1963* (1997) and *Bud, Not Buddy* (1999). He was born in Flint.

John F. Dodge (1864–1920) and **Horace E. Dodge (1868–1920)** started out by building parts for other manufacturers' cars. They went on to produce their own models of cars and trucks. They were born in Niles and did business in Detroit.

Joe Dumars (1963–) was a Hall of Fame basketball player with the Detroit Pistons. He's now president of basketball operations for the Pistons.

William C. Durant (1861–1947) was the founder of General Motors Company. He lived in Flint.

Sarah E. Edmonds (1841–1898) of Flint disguised herself as a man and served in the Michigan infantry during the Civil War. She was known as Frank Thompson.

Eminem (1972–) is a rap musician who moved to Detroit when he was a child. He was born in Missouri.

Annie Etheridge (1844–1913) was a medic for the Union army during the Civil War. She was from Detroit.

Edna Ferber (1885–1968) was an author of novels and short stories. She was born in Kalamazoo.

Gerald Ford See page 86.

Henry Ford (1863–1947) was the founder of Ford Motor Company and helped develop modern assembly lines. He was born in what is now Dearborn.

Aretha Franklin (1942–) is a singer who grew up in Detroit. She was born in Memphis, Tennessee.

Marshall Fredericks See page 73.

Haren Gandhi See page 98.

E. Genevieve Gillette See page 15.

Berry Gordy (1929–) is the founder of Motown Records. He was born in Detroit.

Jennifer M. Granholm See page 81.

Gordie Howe (1928–) is an All-Star hockey player who was with the Detroit Red Wings from 1946 to 1971. He was born in Canada.

Gordie Howe

William Hull (1753–1825) was appointed by President Thomas Jefferson to be the first governor of Michigan Territory, in 1805.

Lewis Thomas Ives (1833–1894) was a portrait artist in Detroit.

Earvin "Magic" Johnson (1959–) is a basketball superstar who spent many seasons with the Los Angeles Lakers. He was born in Lansing.

Louis Jolliet (1645–1700) was a French Canadian explorer who accompanied Jacques Marquette along the Mississippi River.

Albert Kahn See page 115.

John Harvey Kellogg (1852–1943) was a doctor who helped create breakfast cereal. He was born in Tyrone.

W. K. Kellogg (1860–1951) manufactured breakfast cereal. He was born in Battle Creek.

Ring Lardner (1885–1933) was a sports journalist and humorist. He was born in Niles.

Charles Lindbergh (1902–1974) was a pilot famous for making the first solo, nonstop flight across the Atlantic Ocean. He was born in Detroit.

Shelley Looney See page 74.

Joe Louis (1914–1981) was a heavyweight boxing champion. He was born in Alabama but raised in Detroit.

Nancy Harkness Love (1914–1976) was a pilot during World War II. Born in Houghton, she started a flight school at Vassar College in New York.

Thomas Lynch (1948–) is a nationally recognized poet. He lives in Milford.

Malcolm X (1925–1965) was an activist who encouraged African Americans to take pride in their heritage. He was born in Nebraska but lived in Lansing for several years.

Jacques Marquette See page 30.

Stevens T. Mason (1811–1843) became the first governor of Michigan when it gained statehood in 1835. He was just 24 years old when he was elected and remains the youngest governor of Michigan on record.

Elijah McCoy See page 95.

Michael Moore (1954–) is a controversial documentary filmmaker. He was born in Flint.

Michael Moore

Rosa Parks (1913–2005) is considered the mother of the civil rights movement. When she refused to give up her bus seat to a white man in Alabama in 1955, she helped start a bus boycott that made history. In later years, she moved to Detroit and worked in the office of Representative John Conyers.

Patricia Polacco (1944–) is a writer of children's books. She was born in Lansing.

Pontiac See page 32.

C. W. Post (1854–1914) founded Post Cereal Company in Battle Creek. He was born in Illinois.

Harriet Quimby (1875–1912) of Branch County was the first female licensed pilot in the United States. She was also the first woman to fly solo across the English Channel.

Gilda Radner (1946–1989) was a comedic actor. She was born in Detroit.

Della Reese (1931–) is an actor and singer. She was born in Detroit.

Martha Reeves (1941–) is the lead singer in Martha and the Vandellas. This Motown star was born in Eufala, Alabama.

Walter Reuther See page 53.

Fannie Richards See page 66.

Smokey Robinson (1940–) is a soul singer and songwriter. He was born in Detroit.

Sugar Ray Robinson (1921–1989) is considered one of the greatest boxers of all time. He was born in Detroit.

Theodore Roethke (1908–1963) was a Pulitzer Prize–winning poet. He was born in Saginaw.

Rosa Parks

Diana Ross

Diana Ross (1944–) is an actor and singer who was once the leader of the Supremes. She was born in Detroit.

Eliel Saarinen (1873–1950) was an architect who was born in Finland. He designed the campus for the Cranbrook Academy of Art, taught classes there, and served as the school's president.

Loja Saarinen (1879–1963) was a textile artist and sculptor who founded the weaving department at the Cranbrook Academy of Art. She was born in Finland.

Barry Sanders (1968–) was a Hall of Fame running back for the Detroit Lions from 1989 to 1999. He was born in Kansas but now lives near Detroit.

Barry Sanders

Henry Schoolcraft See page 39.

Osama Siblani See page 99.

Tecumseh See page 38.

Danny Thomas See page 72.

Helen Thomas See page 67.

Ruth Thompson (1887–1970) was born in Whitehall. She was Michigan's first woman in Congress, serving in the House of Representatives from 1951 to 1957.

Samuel C. C. Ting See page 103.

Chris Van Allsburg (1949–) is a writer of children's books such as *The Polar Express* and *Jumanji*. He was born in Grand Rapids.

Chris Van Allsburg

Gloria Whelan (1923–) is a children's book writer who lives in northern Michigan. Her book *Homeless Bird* (2000) won a National Book Award.

Stevie Wonder See page 70.

Coleman Young (1918–1997) was the mayor of Detroit from 1974 to 1994. He was the first African American to hold the job.

RESOURCES

BOOKS

Nonfiction

Johnson, Elizabeth M. *Michigan*. Danbury, Conn.: Children's Press, 2002.
Knox, Barbara. *Michigan*. Mankato, Minn.: Capstone Press, 2003.
Matuz, Roger. *Albert Kahn: Builder of Detroit*. Detroit: Wayne State University Press, 2002.
McNair, Joseph D. *Ralph Bunche*. Chanhassen, Minn.: The Child's World, 2001.
Pollard, Michael. *Henry Ford*. Farmington Hills, Mich.: Blackbirch Press, 2003.
Santella, Andrew. *Gerald R. Ford*. Mankato, Minn.: Compass Point Books, 2003.
Schonberg, Marcia. *Michigan Plants and Animals*. Chicago: Heinemann Library, 2003.
Troupe, Quincy. *Little Stevie Wonder*. New York: Houghton Mifflin, 2005.

Fiction

Giff, Patricia Reilly. *Willow Run*. New York: Wendy Lamb Books, 2005.
Pfitsch, Patricia Curtis. *Keeper of the Light*. New York: Simon and Schuster, 1997.
Whelan, Gloria. *Once on This Island*. New York: HarperCollins, 1995.
Whelan, Gloria. *Return to the Island*. New York: HarperCollins, 2000.
Whelan, Gloria. *The Wanigan*. New York: Yearling, 2003.
White, Ruth. *Memories of Summer*. New York: Farrar, Straus, and Giroux, 2000.

DVDs

Discoveries . . . America: Michigan. Bennett-Watt Entertainment, 2004.
Historic Travel US: Michigan Memoirs. Travel Video Store, 2005.
Lighthouses of Lake Michigan. Southport Video, 1999.
Shipwrecks of Lake Michigan. Southport Video, 2001.

WEB SITES and ORGANIZATIONS

Department of Environmental Quality
www.michigan.gov/deq
Learn how Michigan is preserving the environment.

Department of Natural Resources
www.michigan.gov/dnr
Read about the Wildlife Action Plan.

The Detroit Zoo
www.detroitzoo.org
Get information about the Detroit Zoo and the Belle Isle Nature Zoo.

Michigan Government
www.michigan.gov
The state government's official site offers all kinds of information about how the state works.

Michigan History Online
www.michiganhistorymagazine.com
Visit this great site for more on Michigan's past.

Motown Records
www.motown.com
Read biographies of musicians and research the history of Motown.

Rosa and Raymond Parks Institute for Self Development
www.rosaparks.org
Learn more about the program Rosa Parks created.

Travel Michigan
www.michigan.org/travel/
The official guide to visiting Michigan offers some great suggestions.

INDEX

★ ★ ★

12th Street Riot, 57–58, *58*
2-AT aircraft, 101

African Americans, 43, 44, 45, 46, 54, *55*, *56*, *57*, 58, 66, 84–85, *87*
agriculture, 13, 22, 24, 25, 30, 39, 41, 46, *68*, 69, 91, 92, *93*, 94, 99
airports, 102
Albom, Mitch, *71*, 133
Allen, Tim, *72*, 133, *133*
alternative fuels, 60, 98
American Revolution, 32–33, 36
animal life, 16–17, *17*, 17–18, *18*, 21, 22, 28, 115, *115*
Ann Arbor, 42, 64, *74*
apple cider, 69, *69*
Apple Island, 32
Arab American National Museum, 65
Archaic people, 22
Ardisana, Lizabeth, 100, *100*
art, 24, *72–73*
AuSable-Oscoda Historical Society and Museum, 109
automobile manufacturing, 47, *48*, 49, *49*, 51, 52, 54, 58, 59, 60–61, 65, 91, 92, 94–96, 98, 103, 115

Battle Creek, *86*, 92
Battle of Fallen Timbers, 33, 38
Battle of Lake Erie, 38
Battle of River Raisin, 38
Battle of Shiloh, *46*
Battle of the Overpass, 53
Battle of the Thames, 38
Beardslee, Lois, 25, *25*
bill of rights, *77*
birds, 16, 17, 18, *18*
Bloomfield Hills, 73
Boeing Airplane Company, 101
Boeing, William, 101, 133
borders, 7, 12, 14, 36, 38
Brûlé, Étienne, 28, 133
Bunche, Ralph, *57*, *57*
burial mounds, 24, *24*

Cadillac, Antoine de la Mothe, 30, 133
Canadian Shield, 10
Cass, Lewis, 39, 42, 89, 133
Central Lowland, 12, 13
Central Michigan University, *67*
cereal, 91, 92
Champlain, Samuel de, 28, *28*
Chandler, Elizabeth, 44
Cheboygan, 108–109
cherries, 68, 69, *69*, 91, 99, 111, *111*
Cherry corn muffins recipe, 69, *69*
Chrysler, Walter, *47*
circuit courts, 83, *83*
civil rights, *56*, *57*, 135
Civil War, 45–46, *45*, *46*
Civilian Conservation Corps (CCC), 53
climate, 14–15, 92
Cobb, Ty, *74*, 133
Coleman A. Young Municipal Center, *73*
Colonial Fort Michilimackinac, *25*
Confederacy, 45, 46
conservation, 17–19, *19*
construction industry, 49
Conyers, John, Jr., 82, *82*
Copper Harbor Lighthouse, 41
Coppola, Francis Ford, 133
Council of Three Fires, 24
Cranbrook Academy of Art, *73*, 136
Crystal Lake, 14
Curie, Marie, 84
Curtis, Christopher Paul, *70*–71, *71*, 133

DaimlerChrysler automobile company, 91
dance, *73*
Darrow, Clarence, 85
Dearborn, 52, 63, 65, *65*, 101, 114–115
Dearborn Inn, 115
DeBaptiste, George, 44, 45
Dempsey, Dave, 19

Department of Environmental Quality, 81
Department of Natural Resources, 17
Depot Museum, 112
Detroit, 10, 30, 31, 32, 33, 36, *36*, 38, 42, 44, *44*, 49, 51, *52*, 54, *55*, 56, 57, 59–60, *60*, 61, 63, 64, 65, 67, 68, 71, 72, 73, *77*, 79, *79*, 84, 94, 102, 103, 115
Detroit Historical Museum, 115
Detroit Institute of Art, *72*
Detroit Lions football team, *74*, 136, *136*
Detroit Pistons basketball team, *74*
Detroit Red Wings hockey team, *74*, 134, *134*
Detroit River, *43*
Detroit River International Wildlife Refuge, 17–18
Detroit Science Center, 61
Detroit Tigers baseball team, *74*, 133
Detroit Zoo, 115
Dirty Jobs television show, 61
discrimination, 54, *55*
Dodge, Horace E., 95, 133
Dodge, John F., 95, 133
dream catchers, 24, *24*
Dumars, Joe, *74*, 133
Durant, William C., *47*, 95, 133

Eastern Michigan University, *67*
economy, 55, 81, 91–103, 103
Edmonds, Sarah E., 45, *45*, 133
Edmund Fitzgerald (ship), 106
education, 42, 54, 66–67, *67*, 86, *97*
elections, *77*, 78, *86*
elevation, 9, 10, 13
Elijah McCoy Day, 95
Eminem, 70, 134
endangered animals, 17
Engler, John, 78

Erie Canal, 40, *40*
Escanaba, 107
Etheridge, Annie, 45, 134
ethnic groups, 63, *66*
European exploration, 28
executive branch of government, *77*, 80, 81
Exhibit Museum of Natural History, 22

Female Anti-Slavery Society, 44
Ferber, Edna, 71, 134
First Michigan Colored Infantry, 45–46
Fisher Building, 49, 115
fishing industry, 94, 100
Flint, 49, 58, 59, 64, 65
foods, 52, 68, 69, 91, 92, *92*, 113
Ford, Edsel, 72
Ford, Gerald, 86, *86*
Ford, Henry, *47*, 53, 54, 94, 134
Ford Motor Company, *48*, *49*, 52–53, 72, 91, 95, 98, 100, 101, 115
Ford River Rouge Factory Tour, 115
forests, 13, 15, 16–17, 27, 32, 46, *47*, 53, 92, 111
Fort Michilimackinac, 28, 108
Fort Pontchartrain, 30
Fort St. Joseph, 33
Fort Wilkins, 41
France, 7, 27, 28, *29*, 30, 31, 32
Frankenmuth, 113
Franklin, Aretha, 134
Fredericks, Marshall, 73, *73*
Frederik Meijer Gardens and Sculpture Park, 112
Free States, 43
French and Indian War, 31
French exploration, 7, 27, *29*, 30
French settlers, 27
fur trade, 28, 30, 31, *31*, 41, 92

Gandhi, Haren, 98, *98*
gas crisis, *95*
General Motors (GM), 49, 53, 91, 95, 96
Georgian Bay, 28
Gerald R. Ford Presidential Library, 67
Gillette, E. Genevieve, 15, *15*
glaciers, 11, 22
Gordy, Berry, *70*, 134
governors, 36, 39, 42, *77*, *78*, 80, 81, *81*, 82, 85, *87*, 89, 133, 134, 135
Grand Haven, 14, 112
Grand Rapids, 24, *57*, 64, 65, *72*, 92, 102, 112
Grand Rapids Civic Theater, *72*
Grand River, 10, 14
Grand Traverse Heritage Center, 110
Granholm, Jennifer M., 81, *81*
Grayling, 109
Great Britain, 31, 32, 33, 38, *38*, *39*, 53
Great Depression, 51, 52, *52*, 54, 101
Great Lakes, 7, 14, 22, 27, 30, 33, *39*, 40, 68, 69, 100, 102, 103
Great March to Freedom, 56
Great Seal of Michigan, 88, 89, *89*
Guardian Building, 49–50

Hackley and Hume Historic Site, 111
Harrison, William Henry, 38
Hartwick Pines State Park, 15
Haviland, Laura, 44
Henry Ford Museum, 114
Highland Park, *48*
Holland, 63, *67*, 99, 113, *114*
Holland Museum, 113
Hope College, *67*
Hopewell people, 24
Houghton, 110
Houghton Lake, 14, 110
House of Yesteryear Museum, 107
Howe, Gordie, *74*, 134, *134*
Hull, William, 36, 134
Huron mountain range, 13
Huron National Forest, 111
Huron people, 22
Huron-Manistee National Forests, 111

immigrants, 46, 107
Indian agents, 39
Indiana Territory, 35
industry. *See* manufacturing.
insect life, 17
Interlochen Center for the Arts, 73
International Typographical Union, *47*
internment camps, 85
iron industry, 94
Iron Mountain, 107
Islamic Center of America, 65
Isle Royale National Park, 107
Ives, Lewis Thomas, *72*, 134

Japanese Americans, 85
Jefferson, Thomas, 36
Jeter, Derek, *75*
jobs, 46–47, *47*, 49, 51, 53, 54, 58–59, *59*, 61, *97*
Johnson, Earvin "Magic," 134
Johnson, Lyndon, *57*
Johnston, Jane, 39
Jolliet, Louis, 30, 134
judicial branch of government, *77*, 80, 83, *83*, 85

Kahn, Albert, 115, *115*
Kalamazoo, *67*, 92, 113
Kalamazoo College, *67*
Kalamazoo Valley Museum, 113
Keller, K. T., 53
Kellogg, John Harvey, 92, 134
Kellogg, Will Keith (W. K.), 92, 134
Keweenaw Bay, 28
Keweenaw Peninsula, 28, 107
Keweenaw Peninsula National Historic Park, 107
Kid Rock, *70*
King, Charles, 94
King, Martin Luther, Jr., 56, *57*, *57*
Knudsen, William S., 53

La Salle, René-Robert Cavelier, Sieur de, 30
labor unions, 46–*47*, 53, 85
Lake Erie, 9, 10, 11, 14, 22, *39*
Lake Gogebic, 14
Lake Huron, 11, 14, 22, 28
Lake Michigan, 7, 11, 13, *13*, 14, 22, 24, 28, 36, 92, 99
Lake Ontario, 14, 22
Lake Superior, 14, 22, 24, 106, 107
Lambert, William, 44, 45
land area, 10
languages, 40, 65, *65*, 68

Lansing, 42, 64, *72*, *78*, *79*, *87*, 113–114
Lardner, Ring, *71*, 134
laws, 18, 44, 81, 82, 83, 85
Legend of Sleeping Bear (Kathy-Jo Wargin), 78
legislative branch of government, *77*, *78*, 80, 81, 82, 88
Lexington, *68*
lieutenant governors, *77*, 80, 81, 85
lighthouses, 39, 41, 105, 106, *106*
Lincoln, Abraham, 46
Lindbergh, Charles, 101, 134
literature, *70–71*, *71*, *73*, 136
Livonia, 39
local governments, 85–86
Longfellow, Henry Wadsworth, 39
Looney, Shelley, *74*, *74*
Louis, Joe, *75*, 134
Love, Nancy Harkness, 101, 134
Lower Peninsula, 10–11, *11*, 12, 13, 14, 15, 35, 36, 56, 64, 68, 98, 99, 111
Ludington State Park, 15
lumber industry, 15, 17, 46, *47*, 91, 92, 98
Lumberman's Monument Visitor Center, 109
Lynch, Thomas, *71*, 134

Mackinac Bridge, 11, *11*, 56, 61, *61*, 102
Mackinac Island, 28, 36, 38, 105, 108, *108*
Mackinac Island State Park, 108
Mackinac Island's Historic Downtown District, 108
Mackinaw City, *25*, 28, 110
Manistee National Forest, 111
manufacturing, 46, *47*, 48, *48*, 49, *49*, 51, 52, 53–54, 58, 59, 60–61, 64, 65, 91, 92, 94–96, 98, 101, 103, 115
maps
  agriculture, *93*
  counties, *87*
  Detroit, *79*
  French exploration, *29*
  interstate highways, *104*
  mining, *93*
  national parks, *16*
  Native Americans, *23*
  population density, *64*
  statehood, *37*
  territory, *37*
  topographical, *12*
marine life, 16, 69, 100, *100*
Marquette, 30, *67*, 106–107
Marquette, Jacques, 28, 30, *30*
Marquette Maritime Museum, 106
Mason, Stevens T., 42, 135
McCoy, Elijah, 95
Ménard, René, 28
Michigan Agricultural College, 15
Michigan Historical Museum, 114, *114*
Michigan Iron Industry Museum, 107
Michigan Jobs Commission, 81
Michigan Recycling Coalition, 18
Michigan State University, 15, *67*, *72*, *75*, *75*, 114
Michigan Territory, *7*, 36, *37*, 39, 40, 41, 42, 89
Michigan Women's Historical Center and Hall of Fame, 114
Mill Creek Historic State Park, 110
mining, 22, 46, *93*, 107
Mio, 14
missions, 28, 30
Model T automobile, *47*, *48*, 94, 96
Moore, Michael, *72*, 135, *135*
Motown Records, *70*
Mount Arvon, 9, 10, 13
Mount Curwood, 13
Mount Pleasant, *67*
movies, *72*
Mt. Pleasant School, 40
Mulhern, Daniel, 81
Murphy, Frank, 84, 85
music, *60*, *70*, *73*
Muskegon, 111
Myers, Elijah E., *79*

National Association for the Advancement of Colored People (NAACP), 54
national parks, *16*, 107
Native Americans, *22*, *23*, 24, 25, 27, 28, 30, 31, 32, 33, 38, 39, 40, 41, 107, 110
Natural Bridge, *108*
natural gas, 98–99
Nicolet, Jean, 28
Niles, 33
Northern Michigan University, *67*
Northwest Ordinance (1787), 33, *77*
Northwest Territory, 33, 35

Oakland University, 67
Odawa people, 22, 24, 32, *32*
oil, 98–99
Ojibwa people, 22, 24, 25, 39
Olds Motor Company, 95
Olds, Ransom, *47*, 94
Olympic Games, *74*
Oscoda, 109
Ossian Sweet House, *84*

paper manufacturing, 17
Parks, Rosa, 135, *135*
per capita income, *55*, *59*, 103
Pictured Rocks National Lakeshore, 15
plant life, 15
Polacco, Patricia, 135
poll taxes, 54
Pontiac (Odawa chief), 32, *32*, *57*
Pontiac's Rebellion, 32
population, 40–41, *47*, 49, 64, *64*, *65*
Porcupine mountain range, 13, 15
Porcupine Mountains Wilderness State Park, 15
Post Cereal company, 92
Post, Charles William (C. W.), 92, 135
Potawatomi people, 22, 24
prehistoric people, 21, 107

Quimby, Harriet, 101, *101*, 135

R. E. Olds Transportation Museum, 114
race riots, *55*, *55*, *57–58*
Radner, Gilda, 135
railroads, 42, 92, 102
recipe, 69, *69*
Reese, Della, *55*, 135
Reeves, Martha, 135

religion, 28, 30
Renaissance Center, 59–60, *60*
reservations, 41
Reuther, Roy, 53
Reuther, Victor, 53
Reuther, Walter, 53, *53*
Richards, Fannie, 66, *66*
River Raisin, 36
Rivera, Diego, 72
roadways, *11*, 39, 42, 56, 102, *104*
Robinson, Smokey, 70, 135
Robinson, Sugar Ray, 135
Rochester, 67, 72
Roethke, Theodore, 71, 135
Rogers, Robert, 31
Roosevelt, Franklin Delano, 53, 54, 85
Ross, Diana, 136, *136*
Rouge River, *19*

Saarinen, Eliel, 73, 136
Saarinen, Loja, *72–73*, 136
Saginaw Valley, 41
Sanders, Barry, 74, 136, *136*
Sault Sainte Marie, 28, 30, 36, 39, 106
Schoolcraft College, 39
Schoolcraft, Henry, 39, *39*
sea lampreys, 100, *100*
Second Baptist Church, *44*
Seger, Bob, 70
Senate bean soup, 69
service industries, 98, 103
settlers, 36, 38, 39, 40, 41, *41*, 92, 99, 108–109, 113
Siblani, Osama, 99, *99*
Sisters of the Great Lakes, 25
sit-down strikes, 53
slavery, 32, 33, 43, 44, 45, 46
Sleeping Bear Dunes National Lakeshore, 13, *13*, 15
Smokey Robinson and the Miracles, 70
Soo Locks, *103*, 106
sports, *74–75*, *74*, *75*, 86, 98, 133, 134, *134*, *136*
St. Jude Children's Research Hospital, 72
St. Marys River, *103*
state capital, 42, 79, *79*, *87*
state capitol, *78*, 114
state constitution, 67, 77, 78, 81, 85
state flag, 88, *88*
state motto, 89
state nicknames, 9
state parks, 15, 108, 110
statehood, 33, 41, 42, *77*
Sterling Heights, 64
Stout Metal Airplane Company, 101
Stout, William, 101
Straits of Mackinac, 11, *11*, 30, 56. 110
Superior Upland, 12, 13
Sweet, Ossian, 84–85

Tecumseh (Shawnee leader), 38, *38*
television, 61, 72
Territory of Michigan. *See* Michigan Territory.
theater, *72*, *73*, 109
Thomas, Danny, 72, *72*
Thomas, Helen, 67, *67*
Thompson, Frank. *See* Edmonds, Sarah E.
Thompson, Ruth, 82, 136
Ting, Samuel C. C., 103, *103*
Toledo Strip, 41–42
Toledo War, 42
Torch Lake, 14
tourism, 59, 81, 98, 114
Tower of History, 106
transportation, *11*, 39, *40*, 42, 56, 60, 94, 101, 102–103, *102*, *103*, *104*, 106, 114
Traverse City, 110–111
Treaty of Ghent, 38
Treaty of Paris, 33
Tri-Motor aircraft, 101
Tulip Festival, *113*

Underground Railroad, 43–44, *43*, *44*, 70
unemployment, 53, 59, 61, 81, 96
Union, 45
United Auto Workers, 53
University of Michigan, 22, 42, 67, *75*, 86, 103
Upper Peninsula, 10, 11, *11*, 12, 13, 14, 15, 28, 36, 41, 56, 68, 69, 98, 105
Van Allsburg, Chris, 70, 136, *136*
Van Andel Museum Center of the Public Museum of Grand Rapids, 112
Vanderbilt, 14
Vernor's ginger ale, 68
Voigt House Victorian Museum, 112
Voting Rights Act, 57
voyageurs, 30

Wagoner, Rick, 96
War of 1812, 38, 39
Warren, 64, 65
Wayne, "Mad Anthony," 33
Wayne State University, 67, 82
Web sites, 15, 17, 22, 25, 30, 32, 39, 53, 66, 67, 72, 73, 74, 81, 82, 86, 95, 98,99, 100, 103, 106
West Michigan Environmental Action Council, 19
Western Michigan University, 67
Whalen, Gloria, 71, 136
wigwams, 25, *25*
wildlife. *See* animal life; insect life; marine life; plant life.
Wildlife Action Plan, 17
Willow Run Bomber Plant, 54
wolverines, 42
Women's Auxiliary Ferrying Squadron, 101
Wonder, Stevie, 55, 70, *70*
Woodland culture, 22
Woodward, Augustus B., 36
World War I, 48
World War II, 53–54, 85, 86, 101, 111
World's Biggest Cherry Pie Tin, 111

X, Malcolm, 58, 135

Yankee Air Museum, 109
Young, Coleman, 87, 136
Youth in Government, 78
Ypsilanti, 67

AUTHOR'S TIPS AND SOURCE NOTES

★ ★ ★

When I was growing up, every summer vacation meant a trip to Michigan. My family and I would load up the station wagon and head north to Milford, my mom's hometown.

When I was writing this book, I enjoyed my trip down memory lane. But I did lots of research, too. Travel Michigan sent me lots of information about terrific places to visit. I read all about Michigan history. Some of the best books I found were *Michigan: A History of the Great Lakes State* (3rd edition, 2002), by Bruce A. Rubenstein and Lawrence A. Ziewacz; *Michigan Voices: Our State's History in the Words of the People Who Lived It* (1987), compiled by Joe Grimm; and *Michigan: A History of the Wolverine State* (3rd edition, 1995), by Willis F. Dunbar and George S. May. I also used the Internet. I found incredible details at Making of America (www.hti.umich.edu/m/moagrp), a primary source reference at the University of Michigan. The Michigan government site gave me all kinds of facts, and the site for *Michigan History* magazine was amazing! But when I used the Internet, I had to be careful to use sites from respected groups. You should always question where information comes from. So colleges and government sites, as well as museum and library sites, are good ones to trust.

Photographs © 2008: age fotostock/Dennis MacDonald: 114; Alamy Images: 65 (Clark Brennan), 119 (Lynx/Iconotex), 68, 106, 113 (Dennis MacDonald), 121 (Michael Ventura), 28 (Visual Arts Library, London), 19, 59, 62, 63 left (Jim West); AP Images: 83 (Kevin W. Fowler), 127 (Kevin Hare/Battle Creek Enquirer), 77 top, 86 right (Kevin Hare/The Enquirer), 102 (Andy Klevorn/Ludington Daily News), 71 (Carlos Osorio), 84 (Paul Sancya), 120 (John Vucetich/ Michigan Technological University), 15 top; Arab American News: 99; Courtesy of Archives of Michigan: 66; Art Resource, NY/Werner Forman/Field Museum of Natural History, Chicago: 20 bottom; Courtesy of ASG Renaissance: 100 bottom; Bentley Historical Library, University of Michigan: 21 bottom right; Corbis Images: 11 (James L. Amos), 4 top right, 5 top left, 21 bottom left, 34 bottom left, 40, 45, 52, 55, 101, 123, 134 (Bettmann), 103 top (Philippe Caron/ Sygma), 70 (J. Emilio Flores), 135 top (Nicolas Guerin), 33 (Layne Kennedy), 67 inset (Brooks Kraft), 5 bottom, 107 (Lake County Museum), 57 top (David Lees), 50 bottom, 61 (Owaki - Kulla), 129 bottom (Joel W. Rogers), 8, 9 left (Joseph Sohm/Visions of America), 97 (Peter Yates), 27 bottom, 32, 35 top, 39 bottom, 47, 49; Danita Delimont Stock Photography/Chuck Haney: back cover; Dembinsky Photo Assoc.: 9 top, 18 (Dominique Braud), 15 bottom, 126 bottom (Michael P. Gadomski), 4 bottom right, 78 (Gordon R. Gainer), 13 (Howard Garrett), 4 bottom left, 69 top (Doug Locke), 100 top (Gary Meszaros), 4 top left, 17 (John Pennoyer); Doug Meroney Photography: 109; Ford Research & Innovation Center: 98; Getty Images: 133 top (Michael L. Abramson), 74 (Doug Benc), 133 bottom (Michael Buckner), 72 (Arthur Fellig), 136 bottom (Focus On Sport), 136 top (Scott Gries), 58 (Declan Haun), 115 top (Bernard Hoffman), 38 top, 48 (Hulton Archive), 75 (Andy Lyons), 5 top right, 51 bottom, 57 bottom, 124 (Francis Miller), 39 top (MPI), 81, 90, 91 left (Bill Pugliano), 135 bottom (Paul Schutzer), 95 bottom (Allan Tannenbaum), 35 bottom, 94; Gibson Stock Photography: 25 left; ImageState: cover; Index Stock Imagery/Image Port: cover inset; Inmagine: 88, 126 center; iStockphoto: 116 bottom, 130 top (Geoffrey Black), 24 top (Caradore), 130 bottom (David Freund), 128, 129 top (Vladislav Lebedinski), 34 bottom right; Jim West/jimwestphoto.com: 43, 44; JupiterImages: 69 bottom left (Acme Food Arts), 69 bottom right (Susan Kinast); Courtesy of Kellogg Company: 92; Landov, LLC: 53 (CBS), 136 center (Newhouse News Service), 82 (Roger L. Wollenberg/UPI); Library and Archives Canada/ Moorland-Spingarn Research Center, Howard University: 95 top; Courtesy of Lois Beardslee: 25 right; Courtesy of Marshall M. Fredericks Sculpture Museum: 73; Courtesy of National Park Service/ Hopewell Culture National Historical Park: 24 bottom; NEWSCOM: 115 bottom (Detroit Zoological Institute), 112 (Molly Riley/Reuters); North Wind Picture Archives: 46 (Nancy Carter), 20 top, 21 left, 21 top, 22, 26, 27 left, 30, 31, 122; PhotoEdit: 110, 132 (Lon C. Diehl), 51 top, 60 (Dennis MacDonald); Superstock, Inc.: 76, 77 left (age fotostock), 41 (T. H. O. P. Burnham), 50 top, 51 left (Culver Pictures, Inc.), 86 left; The Granger Collection, New York: 27 top, 34 top, 35 left, 36, 42; The Image Works: 108 (Marjorie Farrell), 91 top, 103 bottom (Jim West); UM Photo Services/Scott R. Galvin: 63 top, 67 main; US Mint: 116 top, 118; Vector-Images.com: 89, 126 top.

Maps and Illustrations by Maphero, Inc.